Fishing for the King

James Burn

New Wine Press

New Wine Press
PO Box 17
Chichester
West Sussex PO20 6YB
England

ISBN: 1 874367 60 4

Typeset by CRB Associates, Reepham, Norfolk
Printed in England by Clays Ltd, St Ives plc

Contents

	Foreword	5
	Introduction	7
Chapter 1	The Need for Vision	13
Chapter 2	The Need for Strategy	21
Chapter 3	The Eight-Step Strategy: *To reach lost people . . .*	27
Chapter 4	The Eight-Step Strategy: *. . . and see them transformed . . .*	43
Chapter 5	The Eight-Step Strategy: *. . . into fully devoted followers of Jesus Christ*	57
Chapter 6	Leadership – The Make or Break Issue for the Church	75
Chapter 7	Small Groups – Growing Big by Staying Small	97
Chapter 8	Mobilising the Whole Church for Spiritual Warfare	107
Chapter 9	The God Who Keeps His Word	117

Dedication

To my father, who gave me the passion to write,
to persevere, and to pursue a dream.

Foreword

The message of this book could transform your life and ministry. It is uncomfortably honest and deals with practical issues that are so profoundly simple and obvious but have been constantly overlooked.

We are surrounded by a generation of people who will try just about anything to anaesthetise the reality of their lives; lives which are often meaningless, damaged and empty, faced with the impending reality of death and judgement. The Father loves these people and wants to meet with them so that they can experience His love, grace and forgiveness through Jesus Christ. He wants His Church to be relevant and able to communicate clearly the good news of salvation. God's command to us is to disciple believers that they may become healed, whole, functional human beings. The Father desires that each one should be free to be all that He designed, enjoying their faith and new life in Him, producing fruitfulness for the Kingdom and satisfaction in their own lives. Maybe this book is God's gracious opportunity to help us re-examine our whole purpose, priorities and plans for the future with an understanding of the Father's heart and His true intent for the Church.

James is a powerful communicator and naturally inspirational leader. He often reminds me of Captain Kirk on the Starship Enterprise – a man with faith and vision, willing to go where no man has gone before! Along with his many gifts and abilities, God has placed in James a heart for the lost and damaged, the broken and needy. He is also a family man who seeks to express the Father's love both at home and in the Kingfisher Church, Gloucester, which he and his wife Jan pastor.

James has not only been through the refiner's fiery trials, testing both his faith and character, but seems at times to live in them! Despite this he has not melted away into a pool of despondency or self-pity, but presses on to take hold of his calling.

I believe James is a man set apart for a time such as this. The Church needs men like him who are willing to take risks and break the mould of dead religion to create the new wine skins ready for the new wine of God.

Clive Corfield
Lancaster
December 1996

Introduction

Picture the scene: a mother and her two children go to church regularly. They have been going there for some years, and it has become their spiritual home – they belong, they have made friendships, the children like the Sunday School. Sue's husband doesn't join them as they leave each Sunday morning for church. He doesn't believe in all that – though if Sue and the kids want to believe in that sort of thing, that's fine by him. Besides, he's too busy with other things, like building his business, to get involved. Familiar picture? You've probably got several people like Sue in your church, and maybe, like Sue's friends at church, you're praying for their husbands to make a commitment to Jesus Christ. So what's noteworthy about this true story? Well, one day, Sue's husband found that, because of all the hours he had been putting in to building his business, he had grown apart from Sue and from the children. They were like strangers in the same house. And in his loneliness, he bumped into a girl he once knew, before he'd married Sue. Jane, unlike Sue, was sympathetic and understanding, and Jack found that he could talk to her, whereas with Sue, there was only coldness and distance. One thing led to another, and

Sue and Jack found themselves becoming one more statistic as they sadly went their separate ways.

Does the story still sound familiar? Well, I wonder if you can guess what happened next? Sue, in her misery, turned to her friends at church to find the love and support she needed. After all, that's what church is all about, isn't it – reaching out to those in need, extending the love of Christ to those whose lives are falling apart. But Sue was in for a shock. Instead of the non-judgmental love and support that she hoped for, she was judged, found guilty and rejected. Found guilty of what? Of her marriage failing. How could she, a Christian, be so obviously in rebellion to God? God abhors divorce, and so how could she not forgive her husband and have him back on whatever terms it took, just so long as it stayed out of the divorce courts?

Today, Sue no longer goes to church. Neither do her children. Her ex-husband, Jack, received such condemnation from local church-goers who knew the family that he has grown even more cynical about Christianity. So why is it that the Church is just about the only organisation that shoots its wounded?

Over the last few years I have come across so many who have a similar story to Sue's – people who have, by their own admission, made mistakes and gone wrong, but who have found that, rather than finding God's forgiveness reflected in the treatment they got from church, have found condemnation and rejection. And so, the Church becomes a place of 'pseudo community', where people dare not be vulnerable or 'real', for fear of what might happen to them. But does Church have to be like that? Is it possible to build a church that upholds biblical principles, that does not sell the Gospel short, but does not breed a pharisaic atmosphere?

In fact, it is just this question that led a small group of people to begin to re-evaluate what we do in Church, and, more importantly, who we do it for. I had attended the first Willow Creek conference in Birmingham in 1992, and had been challenged and inspired with a vision of what could be possible if the Church were to take the radical step of actually putting lost people and their needs first. As Bill Hybels is fond of saying, 'Lost people matter to God, and therefore they ought to matter to us.' But what would Church look like if we really took that seriously?

The exploration into that question is the story of Kingfisher – a church for lost and hurting people, who have either not considered Church as featuring anywhere in their search for an answer to life's questions, or who have found themselves further hurt and rejected by Church in the past, when they have no longer been able to keep up the 'party image'.

Kingfisher Fellowship started life in a tyre factory in January 1993. I had been ordained into the Church of England, and had served two-and-a-half years as a Curate. During that time I had been privileged to see many wonderful things happen – dozens of people commit themselves to Christ, the church in which I was serving double in size, and a new congregation planted in a local school. This new congregation was an exciting venture for all of us, especially as, in its early days, it was allowed to be free from many of the religious trappings of the Church of England so as to introduce many of the principles that had been introduced at the Willow Creek Conference in Birmingham. During the first few months of its life, the congregation grew from the original thirty to around one hundred and thirty, with many non-Christians coming along. They were attracted by the 'un-churchy' atmosphere of the services, the talks that were relevant to real life and the innovative children's work – 'The Fun Factory' – based on the theme of the Circus, with two clowns teaching the Christian faith by relating it to life in the Big Top.

It was an exciting time, and left me with a desire to continue to plant such churches all around the city of Gloucester. Sometimes something grips you so much and sets your heart racing at such a rate that you just know that this is a call from God that cannot be ignored. Well, this was one of those occasions, and so, leaving the Church of England, I, and a small group of people with a similar vision, met together in the small back room of a local tyre factory on January 5th, 1993 for the first meeting of Kingfisher Fellowship.

Over the several years that Kingfisher has been in existence, we have experienced a real roller-coaster ride – the joy of seeing people come to faith in Jesus Christ, be set free from emotional hurts, generation ties, destructive soul ties; be released from the occult, be healed from the effects of past abuse. And we have had the pain of those who have walked away from the challenge of developing authentic relationships and being 'real' – coming out from behind the mask and admitting who they really are. The challenges that God has placed in front of Kingfisher are challenges that are facing the Church in general, because the Church is in urgent need of renewal. The issue is not just that we need to fill our churches up with more people so that the long-term decline in church membership is reversed. The challenge facing the Church is to become Good News – to not only offer, but to actually model 'life in all its fullness'.

What does it mean to become that kind of Church? Is it possible for the local church to become the place that has a reputation for welcoming and enabling those whose lives are falling apart, to experience a miraculous change in their lives? Yes it is! God is transforming and renewing His Church today. His desire is that, once again, the Church becomes *'highly regarded by the people'* (Acts 5:13), because it is living the Good News it claims to believe in.

God is challenging His Church today. Will His Church rise to the challenge? Will it actually live the Good News, or will it continue to say 'Do as I say, not as I do?' Rising to the challenges God sets before us, will embark us upon a roller-coaster ride, leaving our 'comfort zones' way behind. There have been quite a few times that we, at Kingfisher, have been sorely tempted to say 'Stop the ride – we want to get off!' But God has persevered with us and we're very glad that He has – and so will you be, as you embark upon this roller-coaster ride – as you rise to the challenge of settling for nothing less that being part of the Church against which *'the gates of Hades will not overcome'* (Matthew 16:18).

Chapter 1

The Need for Vision

'I have a dream!' declared Martin Luther King, on that famous day in Washington. His speech was a defining moment for the United States of America, giving voice to the hopes and dreams of millions of black Americans. He had vision. Hudson Taylor, the great nineteenth-century missionary to China begged God to give him some work to do, 'some self-denying service, no matter what it might be, however trying or however trivial; something with which he would be pleased, and that I might do for him who had done so much for me.'[1] He heard, in return, the voice of God saying, 'Then go for me to China,' and from that moment on the conviction never left him that he was called to bring the Good News of Jesus Christ to that land. He, too, had vision.

'Vision is the art of seeing things invisible,' wrote Jonathan Swift, the seventeenth century satirist, and it is that art – seeing beyond the present situation to a grander future, that enables incredible odds to be overcome. The Bible is full of people with a vision. God gave Abraham a vision – that he would become a great nation – a conduit of God's blessing to all peoples on earth (Genesis 12:2–3). That vision defined the course of his life. Joseph had a vision – that he would become an important and powerful person, reigning over his brothers. His vision kept him going, even when everything seemed to have gone wrong – it gave him the resources to keep going and not be diverted (Genesis 37–50). Margaret Thatcher once commented that people with a vision are distinctive in that 'they go on and on until their goal is obtained.'[2] So vision grips us, points us in a direction, and enables us to overcome seemingly insurmountable odds. As someone once said, 'Only those who can see the invisible can do the impossible.' No wonder people perish without a vision! (Proverbs 29:18 – AV).

So, what's the point of Church? Maybe you have wondered about the answer to that question as you sat through another committee meeting, or realised with horror that this hymn has ninety three verses and nobody (least of all the organist) knows the tune anyway. Well, what **is** the point of the Church? What vision should grip the Church? When I was a boy, I went to church every Sunday, and I got the strong impression that Church was God's instrument of torture. The service only lasted an hour, but it seemed like an eternity, and I would leave saying silently to God, 'You definitely owe me one after that!' It used to appal me that this might be a foretaste of eternal life – imagine being bored rigid for all eternity! I would have been hard pushed to come up with a positive reason for Church being in existence.

And yet, the Church, the community of believers who unite to worship and serve God, is seen in the New Testament as having a central place in God's plans for redemption. In the book of Ephesians, Paul presents the Church as God's New Community – His agent for change in the world, through which Christ makes the two one. He brings ancient enemies – those divided by fear, suspicion, hostility, history, ignorance – into a unifying experience of His grace. The point of the Church, then, is to express that unity to a world of ethnic, social, political and religious divisions; to proclaim boldly that

> *'he himself is our peace, who has made the two one, and has destroyed the barrier, the dividing wall of hostility.'* (Ephesians 2:14)

This unity is, or course, primarily the restored relationship with our heavenly Father, made possible by the death and resurrection of Jesus Christ. Out of that restored relationship flows restored relationships with each other.

Perhaps a harder question to answer is: 'What is the point of **your** church?' What function does it fulfil, and where is it headed? When we started Kingfisher, the pain that many of us felt at the way we had been treated by churches in the past was very raw. Several of us – myself included – had had unhappy and broken marriages, and had felt the pain of not only knowing we had grieved God by our actions, but of feeling the wrath and condemnation of the Church. We didn't want to inflict that kind of condemnation on anyone else, and so we wondered if it was possible to create a church that, rather than shooting its wounded, actually introduced lost, hurting people to the 'God of the second chance?' Could Church be transformational – changing hopelessness, shame and guilt into a real new start with God?

We looked at the New Testament; at how a murderer like Paul became a key player in God's plans; at how a despised tax collector like Levi became a close confidante of Jesus; at how a woman caught in the act of adultery was given the chance to start again by Jesus, and we asked: 'Is it possible to build a Church like that? A place you can go to when your world is falling apart, and find love, acceptance, new hope and transformation?'

As we asked these questions, we felt a growing sense of excitement – a sense of what God's unique 'thumbprint' upon Kingfisher was to look like. But, as Neil Kinnock once said, 'We have to choose between striving for a dream or only being a dreamer,'[3] and so we formalised that vision into the following Mission Statement:

> 'To reach lost people and see them transformed into fully devoted followers of Jesus Christ.'

That is God's thumbprint for our church. It's what we believe God has called us into existence for – to reach lost and hurting people with a love that neither condemns nor condones, but rather shows a better way – shows the possibility of change, and the rich fulfilment of being fully devoted to Jesus Christ.

Formalising this Mission Statement meant that we were committing ourselves to giving priority to the lost – those who are currently outside the Kingdom of God, and those who may have, at some time, expressed some kind of Christian commitment, but who have subsequently lost their way. For us, this Mission Statement has proved to be more than just a management exercise – it has shaped and challenged the very way we do Church. It is amazing how much of Church life is geared towards those already in the Kingdom – the songs we sing (and the fact that we ask people to sing at all!), the words that we use, the expectations we place upon people. When we committed ourselves to reaching lost people, we quickly came to realise that we were committing ourselves to re-thinking just about all of the things we took for granted about Church.

We realised that, if we truly wanted to reach the lost, we had to really appreciate the world the lost live in – the world in which the fundamental concern is not so much being worried about dying as being worried about living. And if we were asking those people to give up an hour on Sunday morning to come to Church, we had to give them a reason for doing so that was more compelling than the pull of washing the car, playing football, reading the paper or staying in bed. We had to admit that our past experience of Church was not something that was likely to drag the average non-Christian out of bed on a cold Sunday morning – and yet, God had gripped us with a vision of the possibility of seeing broken lives made whole and hopeless people transformed. So we resolved to give our lives to building a biblical community where Christianity was so evidently in operation that even the most hardened cynic would find their curiosity getting the better of them.

As the church grew, the number of departments within it increased. We began to realise that it was one thing for a committed core of people to be gripped by a vision and have shared goals and values – but how do you keep that vision alive, when there aren't just twelve people, but one hundred? The number of ministries in the church grew, and we added a drama department, homegroups, prayer cells and so on. We gave each department the responsibility of formulating its own Mission Statement, that would reflect both the overall church Mission Statement, and the unique contribution that that department was to make within the church. Now at every annual meeting, we invite the leader of each department to remind us of their individual Mission Statement, and then sum up how, over the past year, that Mission Statement has been furthered, and what contribution it has made to the overall life of the church, as expressed by the church Mission Statement. This may sound somewhat mechanistic and unspiritual, but if you truly believe that God has given you a vision, then surely it is entirely spiritual to want to stick to it – to respond obediently to the voice that says: *'This is the way, walk in it'* (Isaiah 30:21).

How would you sum up the vision for your church? If you did a survey of your church members and asked them the question: 'Where is this church headed? What are we trying to achieve?' would the average church member be able to give a coherent answer? Perhaps it would be a sobering exercise to try. How about starting with the leadership in your church? Would they be able to articulate the vision that drives your church? Gaining God's vision for your church is not just about the majority agreeing on a good-sounding idea – it's about capturing the heart of God for the unique part your church has to play in His grand plan.

Vision not only motivates and provides direction for the church – it enables individuals within the church to gain a vision of who they are in Christ, and where they fit into the great scheme of things. To be part of a church that knows where it is going, that has a sense of where it fits into God's grand plan, is a faith-stretching and exhilarating experience. If the church is communicating that it is dreaming big dreams, then individuals within it are encouraged to dream big dreams – to cry out to God: 'Where am **I** going? What do you want for my life?' Vision motivates, challenges, provides direction, and is infectious. To be in a faith-filled environment causes our own faith level to rise. To be in an environment where vision is clearly articulated encourages individuals to begin to talk about where God is calling them, in what areas He is challenging them, how they are growing, or where they are feeling weak or under attack.

At Kingfisher, we have the lofty aim of becoming fully devoted followers of Jesus Christ. This challenges every area of our lives, and it has often been said that Kingfisher is not a particularly comfortable place to be. This isn't because the way we present Christianity is so awful (I hope!), but because we continually challenge people to abandon their 'comfort zones' – the places where they feel secure and unchallenged – and go for full devotion: the radical, real commitment of someone sold out to Jesus Christ. As Bill Hybels is fond of saying, 'Ninety-five percent devotion is five percent short.' This has caused some to leave Kingfisher, which is always sad and painful. But it is so heart-warming to come across someone like Karen, who, one year on from committing her life to Christ, said recently 'Coming to Kingfisher and meeting Jesus Christ was the greatest day of my life.' Karen is in the process of transformation, coming from a completely non-Christian background, to being a fully devoted follower of Jesus Christ. She's got vision. She knows where she is going.

As the Psalmist wrote,

> *'Blessed are those whose strength is in you, who have set their hearts on pilgrimage.'* (Psalm 84:5)

How would you describe the pilgrimage of your church, and, within that, of your own life? You owe it to your church and to yourself to discover in prayer God's unique 'thumb print'. The starting point for making that discovery is the realisation that the Church worldwide has received no permission from God to just tread water – the vision Jesus cast in Matthew 28, in the shape of the Great Commission, has yet to be fulfilled, and until it is, the Church is still in pioneering mode, reaching lost people, discipling and baptising them: in other words, seeing them transformed into fully devoted followers of Jesus Christ.

> *'And this gospel of the kingdom will be preached in the whole world as a testimony to all nations, and then the end will come.'* (Matthew 24:14)

Even a cursory glance at church attendance statistics shows how great a task is still before us. What part is the Lord calling **you** and your church to play in hastening the end?

Martin Luther King had a dream – a dream that inspired a nation. To dream is a very scriptural thing – it is a sign of the outpouring of the Holy Spirit (Acts 2:17). As we, just a handful of people, met together at the beginning of 1993, with no money, no influence, and just the back room in a tyre factory in which to meet, we, too, had a dream. We had a dream of a church that welcomed sinners and tax collectors. We had a dream that those same people would be transformed into fully devoted followers of Jesus Christ. Time and time again, we have rejoiced as one lost person after another has realised that dream for themselves. So, what's your dream?

Chapter 2

The Need for Strategy

What is the difference between striving for a dream and only being a dreamer? It's great to have a vision and even better to express that in terms of a Mission Statement, but this is where many people stop. I regularly look in the mirror and see an over-weight, unfit couch potato looking back, and feel a fresh surge of determination to get myself looking like Pierce Brosnan by this time next week – but it never happens. Actually, you can put that down to sheer laziness, but often, we can sincerely believe in the vision we have and work exceedingly hard, but still get nowhere near realising our dreams. Why is that? One fundamental reason is that we have no coherent strategy for achieving the vision set before us.

If your church's Mission Statement is something like: 'We aim to present the Good News of Jesus Christ to every single person in our town,' that's a wonderful aim, but how are you going to achieve it? What is your strategy? How are you going to measure whether all of your hard work is actually getting you nearer to that vision? We don't need to only answer the 'What?' question, but also the 'Yes, but how?' question. We realised at Kingfisher that with just twelve people, two guitars and the short-term loan of a room in a tyre factory, we had to be very strategic about what we were trying to achieve. In fact, as we have grown in numbers, the need to be strategic has grown as well, because the opportunities to get involved in all manner of side-tracks has increased. We realised that, if we seriously wanted to be a church that gave priority to the spiritually lost, we needed to structure the church in such a way that the limited resources we had would be channelled in the right direction. It's amazing how strong the temptation is to talk about reaching lost people, but in reality, gearing the programmes in your church towards the already convinced. Without a strategy that is clearly understood and endorsed by the congregation, the vision never becomes a living reality in your church.

And so, we began to develop a strategy that would enable us to reach non-Christians, clearly tell and show them about Christianity, encourage them to take that step of faith, and, as they devote themselves more and more to following Jesus Christ, embark upon a journey of transformation. We call this 'scoring a goal' at Kingfisher, and it enables us to tell the difference between being fruitful in our ministry and merely growing in numbers or in reputation. This was brought home to us in 1995 in a very painful way. Having outgrown the tyre factory, we had moved to a local school, and began to become known around Gloucester as the 'in' church. We had a high-quality band, great drama, children's work that the children actually raved about, and talks that were relevant to real life. We began attracting disaffected people from other churches, and our numbers went up and up. But people who leave one church with a grudge, and then join another church without working that grudge through, are like living, breathing time-bombs.

Soon, our meetings were packed ... with people who were giving highly-loaded prophecies, who were criticising our 'seeker sensitive' approach as being 'not open to the Spirit', who were attempting to do the ministry they had been denied in their last church. It was a nightmare! And then, people started leaving, and soon the trickle turned into what seemed like a stampede, as, within the space of six months, forty people left the church.

They left because we were too charismatic; not charismatic enough; too preoccupied with reaching the lost; not evangelistic enough; too authoritarian; not strong enough on disciplining people. It was a period of time during which I really wished God had called me to be a minor bank clerk somewhere – anywhere – else. A local Bible College that had just relocated to Gloucester had asked for details about all of the local churches, so that their students could choose which church to attend. More and more of them had begun to come along to Kingfisher, until a quarter of the entire college was attending. It was wonderful to have Christians from around the world in our midst.

Then, one day, I had a phone call from the Principal. The College had received some anonymous phone calls concerning Kingfisher. Unspecified rumours and gossip had been passed on, and on the basis of that, the Principal felt he should instruct his students to give Kingfisher a wide berth. Overnight, all of the Bible College students disappeared, leaving a sizeable hole in the congregation and dealing a severe blow to our reputation. Was it all coming to an end? Those of us who were left felt battered and hurt, wondering if we had got it all wrong, and that perhaps the vision we had was unrealistic and somehow doomed to failure.

We came to see however, that painful though people

leaving is, outrageous though gossip and rumour-mongering is, attracting transfer growth and Bible College students does not actually constitute scoring goals at Kingfisher. It is so easy to equate numerical growth with God's blessing, and, therefore, when people leave, to assume that 'the glory of the Lord has departed.' Numerical growth, if not properly analysed can effectively serve to divert attention away from what God has really called us to.

I am reminded of the Transatlantic rowing race that was held in 1966, which was won by Chay Blyth and Jeremy Ridgeway. It was a great triumph for them, but others were not so lucky. One particular boat, called Puffin, was found capsized in the middle of the Atlantic. Its crew, David Johnstone and John Hoare were nowhere to be found. Johnstone's log, however was still in the boat. In it was a revealing passage:

> 'There is a strange angle to this effort of rowing which we both seem to notice. When things are very discouraging it is hard to find the energy – say when it is important to row against the wind in the first week of the voyage; and when we are swinging along – a hundred miles a day – why bother to add one's puny fifteen or twenty miles?'[1]

Johnstone and Hoare succumbed to the illusion that, because they seemed to be moving along, they need not bother to row, and so they were caught mid-Atlantic in a huge and, tragically fatal storm. Blyth and Ridgeway were under no such illusions and just kept rowing. So it is when we allow ourselves to just be swept along by the current of numerical growth, rather than sticking to the strategy that God gives us to achieving our vision.

Currents come and currents go, and are not to be relied upon. It was one stroke after another that enabled Blyth and Ridgeway to achieve their vision.

If scoring a goal for us was enabling a spiritually lost person to find Jesus Christ, and become free to be transformed into a fully devoted follower of Jesus Christ, our painful experiences of 1995 made us quickly realise that this wasn't just going to happen by chance. Being swamped by 'church hoppers' and attacked by other churches in the area was taking all of our energy, and we were finding less and less opportunity and desire to reach the lost. We needed a strategy that, regardless of which way the current was flowing, would enable us to stay focused on what God was calling us to do. So, through prayer, repentance and a renewed appreciation of what God was calling us to, we introduced an eight-step strategy. This strategy works for us – will it work for you? Probably not if you just take it off the shelf and impose it on your church. It works for us, because it fits in with the particular vision God has given us, and with the particular people He has graciously sent our way. However, there are principles embedded within this particular strategy that I believe are relevant to any situation and in particular to your situation. You don't score goals very often by chance. More often than not, it's by developing a God-given strategy and sticking to it.

Chapter 3

The Eight-Step Strategy:
To reach lost people . . .

Step One:
Equip and encourage Christians to present a compelling witness

There is no evangelistic technique and no church growth insight so powerful as the attractiveness of a changed life. Non-Christians aren't stupid – they can spot a cover-up. They know if the message they are hearing about Christianity is not being lived out in the life of the Christian doing the telling. We have found time and time again that it is not Christianity that non-Christians reject so much as what is being portrayed by Christians. I became a Christian the first time I heard the Gospel. It was in 1980 at an event in the Royal Albert Hall, London, where David Watson gave a clear, concise, easy-to-follow explanation of what it meant to live your life without Christ, what it meant to accept that He died for you; how you could receive Him into your life, and what you could expect to happen as a result. That was the first time I had ever had the Gospel explained to me –

and yet, I had been going to church twice every Sunday for nineteen years! Why is it that Christians find it so hard to clearly communicate what Christianity is all about to their non-Christian friends and neighbours? I am no exception. After becoming a Christian, I joined a lively Anglican church where I was exposed to the phenomenon of the 'bear hunting' season. Once a year, for a couple of weeks during the summer, the dreaded word 'evangelism' was wheeled out and dusted down. We were suitably stoked up through guilt-inducing sermons, with the result that a group of those who had not yet learned to let the guilt bounce off their armour met to go out and do door-to-door evangelism. I endured two 'bear hunting' seasons before my fear and embarrassment outweighed my guilt. I remember my most fervent prayer during the season being, 'O Lord, let my road be the furthest from the church,' so that it would take quite a while for me to get there and back, thus leaving the least amount of time for actually knocking on doors. Needless to say, this was not a tremendously fruitful area of ministry for me, and it left me quite sure that evangelism was not my thing!

I suspect that evangelism sends shivers of fear down the spines of most Christians, because the picture they carry in their minds is one of door-knocking, or street-corner yelling, or embarrassing conversations where they find themselves completely out of their depth in no time. I've experienced all of these forms of 'evangelism', and each one has left me vowing, 'never again!' We were faced at Kingfisher with the dilemma that God had clearly called us to be a church that gave priority to the lost, and yet most of us found evangelism embarrassing and scary. One of the core values of Kingfisher is that, if God made us and gave us a personality, then we should feel free to express that personality. The church should particularly be a place where people can be 'real', find out how God has 'wired them up' and not feel guilty about it, or feel that they ought to be different. If God did not make you a raving extrovert, then surely it is not a failing on your part if you find it difficult to stand up in the middle of the shopping arcade and challenge people to 'turn or burn'.

It is when we recognise that personality is a God-given thing, and not something to be denied or feel sub-standard about, that we can gain a fresh insight into 'evangelism without tears'. In fact, at Kingfisher, we don't talk much about 'evangelism'. Instead we prefer to talk about 'Contagious Christianity' – using your God-given personality to share the Christian faith in the way that best fits how God 'wired you up'. Willow Creek, in their 'Contagious Christianity' course have identified six different styles of evangelism, each one being found in the New Testament. As we applied their insights through a series of seminars at Kingfisher, we found that, once we got rid of the stereotype of one particular form of evangelism from our minds, and realised that there are different ways of sharing our faith depending upon our personality, evangelism took on a whole new meaning. The relief that swept through the church was almost tangible. For some, the confrontational model of direct challenge displayed by Peter in Acts 2, rang bells. For others, it was the intellectual approach that Paul adopted in Acts 17. For others, who felt that they weren't very good at challenging or answering intellectual questions, the testimonial style of the blind man who was healed in John 9 best described what they were good at. My particular style, it emerged, was the relational style, portrayed by Matthew in Luke 5; building relationships that led to deeper things. The Samaritan woman at the well in John 4, who displayed the invitational style – the 'come and see' approach – caused others to sigh with relief at the realisation that what they were able to do was legitimate evangelism and not just a cop-out.

However, it was the last style – the 'service' style of evangelism that Dorcas was noted for in Acts 9 – that was, perhaps, the greatest revelation. Those with the gift of 'helps', who take pleasure in serving and enabling others, often feel inferior to other Christians who have more 'up front' gifts, and perhaps feel the least equipped to 'do evangelism'. Yet here was someone immortalised in the Bible for using her gifts of service to commend the love of God to non-Christians! This was a revolutionary thought to many, and brought a great deal of healing. We have found that when we have affirmed the God-given personal style of a member of the congregation, and encouraged them to use that in reaching out to non-Christians, rather than rounding up guilt-ridden, petrified people for the 'bear hunting' season, remarkable things take place. It becomes possible just to relax and 'be who you are', and, amazingly, bear fruit. In society today, the question being asked is not so much, 'is it true?' as 'does it work?' This is seen in the rapid growth of the New Age Movement and the Occult. People look at results rather than at the price tag, and this is a major challenge for Christianity. That challenge will not be met by forcing people to do things in ways that God did not design them for. It will be met as Christians demonstrate authentic Christianity, and communicate that in the way in which God has 'wired them up'. This has proved to be the case at Kingfisher time and time again. There is nothing quite so contagious as a life in the process of being transformed.

Step Two: Design a Seeker Service

I just couldn't understand it. I had recently become a Christian, and had started attending a little Evangelical Church, where everyone seemed very sincere and friendly. All right, the forty-five minute sermons were a bit of a drag, and the organ, which was made to work by the organist pumping with his knees, should have been given a decent funeral years before, but I was so excited about being a Christian, that none of this seemed to matter. None of my friends at that time were anywhere near the Kingdom of God, but one of them – Jim – was going through a really rough time in his life, and so it seemed natural to ask him to come along to church. Jesus Christ had transformed my life, so surely He would do the same for Jim. All he had to do was be exposed to Christianity, hear the message, and there would be no stopping him. So, one Sunday, I managed to get Jim along to my church. The service went as per normal. The Pastor was in the middle of some sermon series that had been going on for ages, and the talk was the regulation three quarters of an hour. He had this annoying habit of saying, around twenty five minutes into the sermon, 'And finally . . . ', which always gave me false hope that it was about to end. I fell for it every time, and this day was no exception. The hymns were all of the ninety-three-verse variety, and so the service continued for an hour and a half. Pretty normal, I thought. Jim couldn't get out fast enough, and when, a few days later I finally tracked him down and asked him how he had found it, I just couldn't understand his reply. How could he not have liked it? It was about God, wasn't it? God could sort out all of Jim's problems, if only he would let God into his life. So, what was the problem? The problem for Jim, of course, was not God at all – the problem was the church that I had invited him to. How could I, a sane and rational person, sit through **that** every Sunday? How was **that** going to help make sense of Jim's life?

This is a very real issue for many Christians. They are encouraged by their church to get to know non-Christians, share their faith with them, and encourage them to take Christianity seriously for themselves. The problem comes when that non-Christian finally comes to church, either out of curiosity or desperation. They enter into another world, and all-too-often are baffled, discouraged and turned off by what they encounter. This makes the already terrifying prospect of evangelism doubly difficult. Just suppose I pluck up the courage to talk to someone about the Christian faith ... where would I take them to find out more? Sadly, the local church is often the last place where a non-Christian would feel comfortable, or be presented with a compelling case for becoming a Christian. Whether the setting is formal and laden with time-honoured ritual, or more free-flowing and charismatic, the emphasis, all too often, is upon servicing the already-convinced. This leaves the visitor feeling either excluded or over-exposed, often foolish because they didn't know what to do or when to do it, and unhappy about being made to say things that they don't believe.

We realised that, if we were serious about our desire to reach lost people, and were, therefore, asking the members of the congregation to invite their non-Christian friends along, we would need to completely re-think what we were offering on Sunday mornings. We told people, 'If you take the courageous step of sharing your faith with a non-Christian friend or neighbour in whatever way God has wired you up, and you invite them to church, we promise that we will not embarrass you or them, and will commit ourselves to ensuring that everything that happens on each Sunday morning will be with the non-Christian in mind. They may not agree with what we say, or believe the same things we believe, but we will do our utmost not to bore them, confuse them, embarrass them, or cause them to see Christianity as an irrelevance.'

You may well be thinking, 'Well, our church isn't **that** bad!' How about trying the following exercise? Tell someone outside of the church that you know well, that you are conducting an experiment and would really value their help. Would they, for just one service, come along to your church as an observer, and afterwards give an honest opinion about the experience? Did it make sense? Did they feel welcomed, or ignored, or overwhelmed? Did it touch them in any way? What would discourage them from, or encourage them to, come back? If you make it clear they are just helping you with your research, you are less likely to lose a friendship over it, and you may well find it rather illuminating.

Having made that commitment to the people coming along to Kingfisher, we then began to ask ourselves – what **does** it mean to be relevant to a non-Christian? It's very tempting to say, 'we sing modern choruses, have electric guitars and drums, don't wear sharp suits, and we got rid of the pews last year . . . so we must be up-to-date and relevant.' This isn't necessarily so, and can, in fact, make your church less relevant. We found that most people visiting our church still had some kind of memory of religion, and expected to experience some of those memories when they visited the church. The essence of building a church for the un-churched is that we become relevant to them, rather than presenting something to them that we think is relevant and expecting them to flock to us.

And so, using the gifts that God had given us, we began to create the kind of morning service that would reach out to and connect with a non-Christian, without in any way selling the Gospel short. We do not, by and large, live in a 'book culture'. People get their information from the television, the radio, or the tabloids. The most popular TV entertainment on a consistent basis is soap operas, and so, with the help of some talented script writers and actors, we set about writing our own dramas of the soap opera variety, offering a 'slice of life', and highlighting a problem that would then be addressed through the sermon. Most often, God, Christianity and religion in general aren't mentioned in these dramas – they don't have to be. The dramas highlight real-life situations, like marital strife, loneliness, unemployment and so on. They enable the seeker to say, 'yes, that's what **my** life's like. They understand where I'm coming from.'

It is not a natural thing for the average non-Christian to sing, except if they go to a football match. It can make people feel uncomfortable and foolish. However, in coming to church, people often carry that distant memory of singing hymns during their childhood years, and expect a certain amount of hymn singing. We try to strike a balance, by singing both traditional hymns and modern songs, but also having songs sung to the congregation. Our worship leader, Oliver Bennett, is a gifted singer/songwriter, and writes songs that reflect the subject matter of that morning's service. We also make use of secular music, and audio-visual presentations. For instance, recently we were looking at how to strengthen marriage relationships. To underline the place where most people were coming from, we displayed a series of slides of lonely, sad or angry people whilst playing Elton John's 'Sorry seems to be the hardest word'. It was a very powerful statement of where many relationships were that morning, and poignantly set the scene for the following talk, about truth-telling, giving and receiving forgiveness and making the shrewd investment of time. People went away from that meeting with a fresh determination to set wrong relationships right, and several took a step nearer to the one relationship that matters above all others.

The talks we do in these services are not just pandering to peoples' neuroses – we pull no punches in talking about God's love, His holiness, His righteousness, His justice, or the radical nature of a true commitment to Christ. But we approach these truths from the real-life situations that the average non-Christian finds themselves in. A recent series we did was entitled: 'Unravelling the religious maze', and looked, over six weeks, at the major alternatives to Christianity, at their distinctive beliefs, at where they differ from Christianity, and at why Christianity is the wisest choice. One particular person, who was very attracted by the New Age Movement, and is doing and MA in ecology, was intrigued by this series – particularly on the talk entitled 'The New Age Movement – The Age of Aquarius'. He started coming to church to hear what we would have to say on the alternatives to Christianity, and now says that his life has taken on a whole new direction as a result.

One of the major keys to successfully encouraging the members of the congregation to take the risk of talking to their friends about Christianity, is this commitment to produce a weekly service that they know their friends will enjoy. Is that merely entertainment? Certainly that is a charge that has been levelled at us. However, these services are very challenging indeed, often leaving people in tears, and sometimes even making them run out of the building, unable to cope with the reality of what is going on. But often there is much laughter and enjoyment, and we feel that this is the kind of atmosphere where people will be most open to receiving truth and doing something about it. Do you need to have gifted songwriters, actors, or multi-media experts to make it happen? We had none of these people when we started – they were attracted by what we were trying to achieve. The essential thing is you deciding how important lost people are. Does it really matter that, with churches all around them they are headed for a Christless eternity? And if it does really matter – what's **your** church going to do about it?

Step Three:
Encourage Team Evangelism

We often get people just coming to take a look at Kingfisher. Either they are visiting the area, taking a break from their own church, or are non-Christians beginning their journey towards becoming a Christian. One particular woman had been visiting for a few weeks, and I never quite seemed to catch her to say hello. She seemed to be at ease during the service, but dashed off at the end. I decided to race her to the door one Sunday morning and at least say 'Goodbye' before she escaped. I finally managed this, and got into a conversation with her which was very illuminating. She appeared to be a confident, articulate, career woman, who knew her own mind, and was used to competing in the market place. As we talked, she revealed that she had been wanting to come to our church for over a year, ever since she had received some of our literature through her door. However, she just hadn't been able to pluck up the courage to come. In fact, it wasn't until her mother, who had just started going to church herself, happened to be visiting her one weekend and agreed to accompany her, that Joanne plucked up enough courage to come along. She was now very glad that she had, and soon after that conversation, gave her life to Christ and is now busy encouraging others to come along.

It brought home to me just how difficult it is for non-Christians to cross the threshold of a church, however confident they may appear to the casual observer. Those who do take the plunge have their defences up. Will they be made to feel embarrassed? Will they be ignored? Will they become the centre of unwelcome attention? Will it be like one of those time-share sales meetings, where you don't get out alive without agreeing to buy something you don't want? At the same time, these people are assessing what they are seeing, what they are hearing, and the way people are with them, as part of their assessment of whether Christianity is for them or not. More than that, if they had trouble parking their car, finding a seat, hearing or seeing, they are forming a negative opinion, not only of this particular church, but even of Christianity in general. We too often do not see church through the eyes of a visitor, and we therefore fail to appreciate that it is not just the content of the message or the composition of the band that will or won't bring them back, but the whole experience, from the time they were invited, to how they are followed up afterwards.

This realisation has led us to emphasise the concept of Team Evangelism at Kingfisher. Whilst we are all called to present a compelling witness to our non-Christian friends and neighbours, we all have a role to play together to ensure that a non-Christian visitor is shown the best of Christianity while they are on our premises. Team evangelism is about the whole church playing their part, whether that is giving out notice sheets, helping in Action Pack, our children's work, participating in the service, serving tea and coffee afterwards, or helping on the bookstall. Each area of service has a crucial part to play in commending Christianity to a visitor. If they feel welcomed without feeling overwhelmed when they arrive, if their children are well looked after, if they are talked to after the service without being made to feel pressured; all these things are vital components of evangelism, and enable the whole church to participate. One person may not be able to answer the questions their non-Christian friend is asking, but they know that there is someone at church who can. Another person may feel that their gift of Helps is of little use in bringing someone to Christ. In fact, for a visitor to be put at their ease by being efficiently shown to an empty seat, given a cup of coffee afterwards, and engaged in 'safe' conversation, is a vital part in the chain of events that constitute the process of becoming a Christian. In God's kingdom there are no spare parts:

> *'The eye cannot say to the hand, "I don't need you." '*
> (1 Corinthians 12:21)

So it should be in the Church. We are all vital parts in God's plan to reach lost people and see them transformed into fully devoted followers of Jesus Christ.

Whilst I was in Chicago in 1994 visiting Willow Creek Church, they were in the midst of some atrocious weather conditions. The snow was piled high, the temperature was around –20°C, and driving conditions were very dangerous. All week, as conference delegates arrived at and left the church, a small army of car park attendants spent hours in the freezing conditions, directing traffic. At the end of the week, I met one of them with his family in the restaurant area of the church. I asked him why on earth he did what he did – surely it was rather above and beyond the call of duty, spending a whole week out of what must have been his annual holiday entitlement, in order to stand in sub-zero temperatures directing traffic. Here's what he said. 'When visitors come onto the Willow Creek campus, I am often the first person they meet. On their spiritual journey of assessing whether Jesus Christ is for them or not, I am, perhaps, the first link in that chain of events. If I do my job well, they will be encouraged to enquire further, and hopefully, one day, commit their lives to Jesus Christ.' That's Team Evangelism. Do people in your church just do jobs because they've got to be done – or are they participating in the greatest enterprise known to mankind: commending Jesus Christ to lost people in their own unique and vital way? Casting the vision of Team Evangelism mobilises and energises the whole church for service.

Step Four:
Encourage Seekers to attend an Enquirers group

One particularly exciting development in Church life in the UK of recent years, has been the emergence and development of evangelistic small group courses such as Alpha, which has been developed by Holy Trinity, Brompton. It provides the tools to reach out effectively to non-Christians and offer them a coherent and compelling introduction to the Christian faith.

However, the introduction of an Enquirers course needs to be seen within the context of an overall strategy for reaching the lost and encouraging them into an on-going pattern of transformation and discipleship. As much attention needs to be given over what the next step for the new believer will be to ensure their continued growth in the Christian life, as to actually getting them to attend an Enquirers group in the first place. Just introducing an Enquirers group into church life which is divorced from an overall strategy of encouraging on-going discipleship can be like sewing a new patch of cloth onto an old garment – the two just do not go together. The Enquirers group could be presenting the Christian faith and radical call to full devotion to Jesus Christ, which just is not reflected in the life of the rest of the church. We seek to create an atmosphere of openness and acceptance which encourages people to ask the questions that are really bugging them about Christianity, religion, the Church and so on. This openness and acceptance, to be real, needs to be a reflection of the general atmosphere of the church. If the Enquirer has seen for themselves over the previous weeks as they have visited and observed what is happening in the church, that it is all right to be real and to admit to personal struggles and doubts, then they are going to feel emboldened to adopt that attitude in the Enquirers group. If, on the other hand, they have observed that there is a party line to toe, with a lack of acceptance and compassion for those who are not currently 'living in the victory', then either the Enquirers group becomes a place of 'pseudo community' where the real questions are never asked and the real issues never addressed, or the group becomes a pressure point in the church, with tensions arising between that group and the wider church leadership. Either way, the church is not encouraging the birth of disciples and is not modelling what it means to be a fully devoted follower of Jesus Christ. I am convinced that what God really wants to do is follow Valerie Singleton's approach, point to the church that the Enquirer is getting involved with, and say, 'Here's one I did earlier! They are living what you are being taught. It works for them, and it can work for you.' Sadly, this is often not the case.

Jesus once accused the Pharisees of going to extraordinary lengths to win a convert, and having done so, weighing them down with impossible demands. Without the clearly stated vision of creating followers who are fully devoted to Christ, the Church can easily fall into the same practice. We are not very good at accepting people for who they are – we tend to want to make them like ourselves. The Church has a long history of this, whether one looks at the way black immigrants were treated by churches in post-war Britain, or how converts arising from the Jesus Movement were treated in the United States, to how single parents are treated today. All too often, initiation into the Christian faith becomes initiation into the value system and social outlook of the church. However, disciple-making is about being the mid-wife who delivers the baby that bears the resemblance of the Father, not the nursing staff!

Evaluation points

- In what ways are the Enquirers groups in **your** church part of a coherent strategy to produce disciples?
- Would you say that the majority of your church is living out what is being presented to the Enquirers in your church, or are your Enquirers groups like a 'new patch sewn onto an old garment'?

- Is your church in the business of presenting the Good News of Jesus Christ to Enquirers, or more concerned with creating good 'club members'? Maybe it's time for a review!

Chapter 4

The Eight-Step Strategy:

...and see them transformed...

Step Five:
Setting the captives free

The events of 1995 just about finished me. I was at a low ebb in terms of self-esteem and felt rejected anyway, and with all the people leaving the church and the increasing amount of malicious gossip surrounding the church, I was beginning to feel that I couldn't take any more. We had announced our intention in January 1995 of planting another Kingfisher church late that year, had identified the person we felt God was calling and equipping to lead that church, and had started to build a team that would be commissioned and sent out. However, this too, suffered a setback, when the potential leader announced that he felt unhappy with the whole notion of Church being for the Unchurched. The Elders and I attempted to talk this through with him, but to no avail, and the following week, without any warning, he and his wife left the church to set up his own their own church in his front room. This had a devastating effect on an already unsettled church, especially as several others left to go with him. I felt a complete failure – the church was falling apart, I had failed to discern the true intentions of this man, and people I cared deeply about were leaving. Because we, as a leadership, felt it wrong to speak publicly about some of the issues in peoples' private lives that were causing them to leave the church, the blame for their departure naturally fell on me. It must have been some issue they had with me; I must have upset them in some way. I was feeling worse and worse, and then came the incident with the local Bible College, and I felt washed up. The cost was no longer worth it. I had had enough – God could find someone else.

However, although I was finished with God, He wasn't finished with me. On the day that the Bible College Principal visited me to say that he was removing his students from Kingfisher – the very day that I reached the end of the road – the phone rang. It was Ellel Ministries, an organisation that exists to bring the healing and deliverance ministry into the local church. They were running a leaders' conference the following month, to encourage and minister to church leaders who were going through hard times, and had just been phoned by someone from Kingfisher church who wished to remain anonymous, and who wanted to book Jan and me into the conference. Would we like to go? I could have wept. This could only have been God – I had told no one else about the visit from the College Principal. No one else knew my depths of despair. I felt like Elijah may well have felt in 1 Kings 19, when he had just finished telling God how very zealous he had been for Him, and how he was the only one left, and how he had had enough, and God gently pointed out to him that life was not as bleak as he was painting it. Maybe God hadn't abandoned us after all. Maybe He would yet do something about the situation.

Jan and I attended the conference, which proved to be an amazing turning point for us. Not the conference itself so much, but through a 'chance' encounter with one of the teachers at Ellel, Clive Corfield. It was one of those fleeting moments that seems at the time to be so casual, but proves to be one of those God-ordained, highly significant moments. I was having one of my 'It's not fair!' conversations with God. There had been some powerful ministry going on, during the course of which a wonderful, healing, uplifting prophecy was given about a leader who was suffering rejection and disappointment, but not to worry because God was about to sort it all out. I was busy thanking God for His goodness, when the recipient of the prophecy was identified as being the person sitting just behind me. I couldn't believe it! How could God miss? Then there was another word that I would have killed for – and that went to someone right on the other side of the room! So there I was, during the coffee break, having my 'It's not fair! What's the point?' conversation with God, when Clive walked past, and said, 'Hello – everything OK?' As he continued walking, I said, 'Well...,' and Clive stopped, turned and said, 'So what's the problem?' I found myself beginning to tell him about how desperate I felt, and how I just couldn't go on. I was angry, disheartened, rejected, and felt a complete failure. Clive could see that I was in a bit of a state, and so we arranged for a time when we could talk further and pray together.

That time happened several weeks later, and proved to be two days of the most intensive, life-transforming prayer I have ever experienced. I knew that I felt angry and rejected and a total failure, for obvious reasons.

Nobody could have gone through what I had gone through over the past three years and not feel how I now felt. But as Clive prayed for me, it began to become apparent that the problems went back far further, into my childhood, right through my family. Rejection was a dominant theme, running from one generation to another. I began to see that so many of my thoughts and actions stemmed from the fear of rejection, and, from that, how often I actually **was** rejected. This had opened the doorway in my life to a spirit of rejection, which drove me to self-pity and the desire to please others and be liked by them – something I routinely failed to achieve. However, whatever anyone said about me that was negative, I willingly embraced, because it fed my self-condemnation and my dislike of myself. I realised that, when anyone left the church, I took it as a personal statement of what they thought about me, and it fed my sense of rejection, my self-pity, my sense of failure. My first marriage had ended in failure, despite all attempts to save it, and this reinforced my sense of rejection and failure. The enormous amount of criticism and condemnation heaped on me by other Christians had led me to a nervous breakdown. I was a total mess! I had gone to Clive hoping for a word of encouragement – you know the sort: 'I, the Lord know of your trials, but fear not – hang on in there, because I will rescue you.' Please understand, I am not belittling that kind of word from the Lord, but I quickly came to realise that He had a far deeper work in mind than just patting me on the back and encouraging me to limp along to the next crisis. I spent two days weeping, as Clive sensitively prayed for me, releasing me from the grip of rejection, self-rejection and the fear of rejection. This enabled me to speak out forgiveness to all those who had hurt me, either on purpose or inadvertently. I felt that every aspect of my life was being re-built, as God took out all the defective parts, threw them away and fitted me with new ones. I walked away from those two days of ministry feeling like I had just been pummelled by Frank Bruno over the full fifteen rounds. It took me days to recover, but when I did, a strange thing happened.

Soon after this time of ministry, I was invited to go and do some teaching in Sweden, which turned out to be a very fruitful and encouraging time. As soon as I returned from that, the church was booked to go away for a weekend to mid-Wales. This proved to be the most incredible experience. I was teaching that weekend on the theme of Renewal, and I felt a completely new sense of freedom and authority in my ministry. The church were rather taken by surprise at the change that had come over me. The Holy Spirit moved very powerfully among us that weekend, showing people areas of their lives that needed healing, patterns of behaviour that were not honouring to Him and were damaging to them, and ministering to people at a deeper level than we had ever experienced before. The consensus of opinion on that weekend was, 'We don't know what it is you've got, but we want it too!' It taught me a valuable lesson about the reality of spiritual covering. Just as Christ is the spiritual covering of the Church, and a husband is the spiritual covering for his family, so a Minister is the spiritual covering for his congregation. That spiritual covering can be likened to an umbrella. If the umbrella has holes in it, the rain gets in and people get wet. Likewise, if the spiritual covering afforded by the Minister is weak and threadbare, because his or her spiritual life is weak and threadbare, then his or her congregation is going to get rained on. They are going to be vulnerable to spiritual attack, and be spiritually weak.

This was so at Kingfisher – people were continuing in sinful patterns of living, unable to kick destructive habits. There was sexual sin in the church and the giving was lack-lustre – we were in a mess. It was a mess that was being perpetuated and allowed by my mess. As I received ministry and allowed God to bring real healing into my life, the effect on the church was amazing. People gave up smoking. The giving went up dramatically. People started confessing their sins, admitting to problems that had been buried and denied for years. Bill Hybels has coined a phrase, 'Speed of the leader, speed of the team', and how true this has proved to be in our situation. I am ashamed at how long I allowed my own situation to go on without receiving ministry, and, as we began to share the insights gained through Ellel Ministries within the church, the major reaction was, 'Why wasn't I told about this when I became a Christian? I now understand why I have struggled so much all these years.'

That's a good question. Why aren't people told about the need to be set free from the past when they become a Christian? We are taught that,

> '*. . . if anyone is in Christ, he is a new creation; the old has gone, the new has come!*'
>
> (2 Corinthians 5:17)

This is undeniably true. However, no one comes to Christ out of a vacuum – each of us carries the effects of our previous life-styles, or the life-styles of the families we grew up in, or even our more distant relatives. The occult pervades many schools today, with séances, ouija boards, 'stilling' and other demonic practices taking the place of smoking behind the bike sheds. So often when people make a decision to follow Jesus Christ, they find that they cannot follow it through, because they have not been set free from their past. To use an analogy, if someone has been smoking heavily for years, their health is seriously at risk. If they then give up smoking, that has got to be a good thing, but it doesn't address the damage caused to their lungs by the years of smoking. They are still going to feel short of breath, have a bad cough and maybe more serious consequences, even though they no longer smoke. The same is true in the spiritual realm.

Anne's family were all, to one degree or another, involved in the occult. They routinely consulted a medium, and one of her brothers practised Transcendental Meditation. At school, Anne had a group of friends who experimented with a ouija board, and Anne joined in with them sometimes. On one occasion, Anne remembers sitting in front of a mirror in her bedroom, reciting the Lord's prayer backwards. She fell into a trance, and when she awoke, she saw that the cross she wore on a chain around her neck had been twisted out of shape by some unseen force. Several years later, Anne became a Christian, and, initially made great progress. However, she began to have nightmares; dark shapes would appear in her bedroom, voices that told her she was going to die. She felt a rising knot of terror inside her. How could this be? She was a Christian now. She struggled on in this manner for several years before coming to Kingfisher. Finally she received ministry, in which she renounced the occult practices she had opened herself up to, and was delivered from the various spirits that been allowed access to her life. Anne is now, for the first time, beginning to know the truth of Jesus' words:

'If the Son sets you free, you will be free indeed!'
(John 8:36)

As we came to appreciate more and more that no one is a completely blank piece of paper when they enter the Kingdom of heaven, we began to realise why it is that so many who make a seemingly whole-hearted commitment to Christ fall away soon afterwards, feeling defeated and disappointed. We began to minister healing and deliverance to people at the point that they became Christians, setting them free from the consequences of their past lives, in order that they be free to grow in the Christian faith.

Peter, for instance, was, to all intents and purposes a successful man. He had got to the top of his profession, was very fit through working out at the gym four evenings a week, had a lovely wife and three children. However, Peter was not interested in getting involved much at church, even though he was a Christian, because he was too busy with his career and fitness schedule. After a while of being at Kingfisher, he was able to ask for help regarding his attitude to his three boys. He had a bad relationship with them, being harsh and aggressive, bullying them to do better at school, to be more sporty, to improve in all areas. He said that he knew what he was doing, and hated it – he just seemed powerless to do anything about it. As we talked, I asked him about his own father, and about how Peter related to him. Peter said that his father had never encouraged or praised him, but had constantly compared him unfavourably with his elder brother. His elder brother had gone to university, but Peter was not considered bright enough. As a result, Peter had vowed not to let his parents – or anyone for that matter – close to him again. He would become hard, successful, 'professional', but the real, hurting, vulnerable Peter would remain undetected. In addition, he formed a 'bitter root judgement' about his father. He hated his father for being so cold and uncaring towards him, and formed a judgement of him on that basis.

However, it is a spiritual principle that you reap what you sow (Galatians 6:7). Peter had judged his father for being a harsh, demanding, unloving man, and so he was due to reap that judgement that he sowed, which proved to be the case when he himself became a father. However, another spiritual principle is that:

> *'They sow the wind, and reap the whirlwind.'*
>
> (Hosea 8:7)

That is to say, what we sow is increased when it is returned to us. The principle of increase is demonstrated in the Parable of the Sower (Mark 4:8), and was in effect, in a negative way, in Peter's life. He had become like his father, only worse. He'd prayed about it, asked God to help him, but nothing seemed to happen. As we prayed together, I broke the power of that bitter root judgement in operation in his life and the power of that inner vow that he had made. Free from those things that had bound him, Peter has been able to move forward in building a new relationship with his sons, starting with him admitting to them what he had been doing, and asking their forgiveness.

Helen, when she started visiting us, had sampled just about every spiritual practice apart from Christianity. She had been involved in spiritualism, palmistry, automatic writing, had had some bad experiences with all of that, so had gone for an 'aura cleansing', had been involved with Tarot cards ... the list went on! Now, she felt so desperate, she came to us as a last resort. As she heard more and more about Christianity, and about the life of freedom from fear that Jesus was offering, she realised this was what she had been searching for all her life. She joined an Enquirers group, and committed her life to Christ. But did she live happily ever after? Absolutely not! She started having horrifying nightmares, featuring ghostly apparitions, and one night when she was not asleep, she actually saw a snake slithering towards her, with huge, horrifying teeth! As she embarked on the 'Setting the Captives Free' course, we took her through the usual questionnaire, where we ask people to tick off all the occult practices listed that they have been involved with. She ticked just about every one. Each one was an 'entry point' for the demonic – a kind of neon sign, flashing 'Come on down!' offering the legal right of residence. We led Helen to renounce all of those occult practices, thus denying them further legal right to have a hold on her. We then rebuked them and commanded them to leave in Jesus' name, and Helen was powerfully delivered and set free, thus giving her the opportunity to move on in the Christian life. Although she still has her struggles, she is going strong in the Christian faith, and is about to be baptised.

Bitter root judgements, inner vows, entry points for the demonic; we were learning as we went, amazed at what God was showing us, and at how He was enabling us to minister to people who, on the surface, looked so 'together', but who were struggling on the inside. For the first time, we were seeing real transformation on a regular basis as people gave their lives to the Lord. We now see it as entirely natural to take people through this course at the point of conversion. How else will people be free to become fully devoted followers of Jesus Christ, unless they are enabled to see real transformation in their lives?

We also learned about the power of words spoken over people – pronouncements and curses. How wrong the old saying is, 'Sticks and stones may break my bones, but words will never hurt me!' Words are powerful, and we hurt people with them on a regular basis. Words can lodge in our inner being and form the basis of the direction of our lives. 'You're just like your mother!' can be a compliment, but more often than not is said to hurt. If the mother in question was a dominant or manipulative person, those words can act as a pronouncement on a person's life, ensuring that, sure as eggs are eggs, that person **does** turn out just like that. 'All the men in this family die young, so I shouldn't think you'll live beyond forty' is a curse that has led more than one person to an early grave. As we started to teach about the power of words, we began to realise just how many curses we rain down upon ourselves and others. 'I'm so stupid', 'Just wait until your kids hit teenage years, then all hell will break loose', and so on. We need to teach people, without becoming superstitious about it, to break the power of those words that have served as pronouncements or curses, over their lives.

'Setting the Captives Free' has proved to be an absolutely crucial element of the strategy that is seeing lost people become transformed into fully devoted followers of Jesus Christ. We still have much to learn in this area, but we are convinced that it is at the point of conversion that people most need to be set free from the chains that bind them. We are also convinced that there isn't a demon under every stone, although the demonic is all too real. Most people aren't so much riddled with demons, as emotionally damaged, and need to undergo emotional healing. However, emotional damage presents a potential entry point for the demonic, and the demonic will often take advantage of that if the emotional damage is not addressed.

Joan, for example, came to us emotionally damaged. She had been repeatedly raped over a period of time by a man; an extremely traumatic experience. To cope with this, she had learned from a friend how to 'switch off' her mind from her body through meditation. This helped her cope with the shock and trauma of her experiences. She began to suffer from all sorts of physical ailments. As we prayed with her, we prayed into the emotional pain of the sexual violation. We lifted from her the spirit of shock and trauma, which allowed the suppressed pain and emotion to surface, enabling real healing to occur, and which had a very beneficial impact upon her physically.

Nobody becomes a Christian out of an emotional or moral vacuum – we all have baggage that needs to be dealt with. However, the Church tends to encourage all of that to be swept under the carpet through an over-simplification of the truth that Jesus Christ is the answer to all of our problems. Indeed He is, but it is crucial that we allow His healing power to touch every area of our lives, and that we realise that past actions and attitudes have consequences that need to be dealt with, in order that we may truly begin to experience 'life in all its fullness'. Healing and deliverance at the point of conversion needs to be a part of the strategy of the Church in reaching lost people, if we truly want to see people becoming fully devoted followers of Jesus Christ, rather than just Church attendees.

One couple started attending Kingfisher who had been Christians for around fifteen years. Prior to that, they had been Jehovah Witnesses. They had made a whole-hearted commitment to Christ, and had become settled in their church. However, they both had great difficulty in accepting the authority of the Bible, and had always found it hard to pray. Their commitment as Christians began to wane, and they eventually stopped attending church. As we prayed for them, God revealed that they had never renounced the beliefs of the Jehovah Witnesses, and neither had they formally renounced the authority that they had allowed the JWs to have over their lives. Consequently, the false teachings they had formerly given credence to, still had a spiritual authority in their lives, even though, on a rational level, they would both have said that they no longer believed in all that. As we broke the power of that false teaching, and as they formally renounced the authority of the Jehovah Witnesses over their lives, they both experiences a sense of release and freedom. They have since started to pray with each other again, and have found a new sense of excitement and fulfilment about the Christian life. Their comment at the end of that time of ministry was, 'Why weren't we told about this fifteen years ago?' Good question! Why is the Church not ministering in this way, 'setting the captives free' as they commit their lives to Christ? Jesus promised that

> *'If the Son sets you free, you will be free indeed.'*
> (John 8:36)

He has been quite honest and open about His desire that the captives be set free, and has said that all that needs to be bound or loosed already has been in heaven – that simply needs to be reflected here on earth. So why does the Church continue to be satisfied with its members being crippled by rejection, guilt and fear, moulded and warped by inner vows, bitter-root judgements, pronouncements and curses, and stunted in their growth by the consequences of the past. Is it not time that the Church began to tell the truth about the Good News of Jesus Christ – that it is not just words, but, as St Paul found at Corinth,

> *'My message and my preaching were not with wise and persuasive words, but with a demonstration of the Spirit's power, so that your faith may not rest on men's wisdom, but on God's power.'*
>
> (1 Corinthians 2:4–5)

Chapter 5

The Eight-Step Strategy:
...into fully devoted followers of Jesus Christ

Step Six: Discipleship

Have you noticed that Jesus, as He gave His disciples their marching orders in Matthew 28, did not command them to go and make conversions, but to go and make disciples? (Matthew 28:19) This says two things to me – that Christ directed His Church to be about the business of encouraging people into full devotion towards Himself, and that the process doesn't happen by accident. Disciples need to be made, because they don't make themselves. Left to their own devices, a 'good' church member becomes 'like a good club member: he attends the club, pays his dues, and tries not to embarrass the club', according to Juan Carlos Ortiz.[1]

The whole subject of discipleship has become very charged, with the rise of the 'Shepherding Movement', and the abuses surrounding Heavy Shepherding. While many churches that were practitioners of Heavy

Shepherding have turned away from this, the wounds that were inflicted through being manipulated and abused are still all too real for many. However, as someone once said, 'The correction for abuse is not disuse, but proper use'. The pendulum swing in many churches today has been too severe, with very little coherent Christian teaching aimed at feeding the new Christian and ensuring they grow in a healthy balanced way. There is a rightful thirst for the reality of the power of the Holy Spirit in our meetings, but all too often this leads new Christians to a feelings-based faith, where I know God is real because of the thrill I get when I'm at church, and because of all these people being 'slain in the Spirit'.

Please understand, I am not knocking charismatic manifestations of God, nor am I saying that it is wrong to feel the whole range of emotions in our walk with God. However, as David Watson has pointed out,

> 'The vast majority of Western Christians are church-members, pew-fillers, hymn-singers, sermon-tasters, Bible-readers, even born-again-believers or Spirit-filled-charismatics – but not true disciples of Jesus.'[2]

It is my belief that the problem lies, not so much with the new believer, but with the Church. We may have 'bear hunting' seasons, or we may be more enlightened and have a coherent strategy for encouraging our members to befriend and invite non-Christians to a Christian event. We may even have a strategy in place for enabling them to take that step of faith and say 'Yes' to Jesus Christ. But then what? So often, we just expect that the new Christian will miraculously know how to pray, or read the Bible, or how to give financially, or what Spiritual gifts are, and what theirs are in particular. We do not see the Church abounding in true disciples, because we are not obeying the command of Jesus Christ, to go and **make** those disciples. If God was going to do it miraculously, why did He instruct His disciples to go and do it? Surely it is the role of the Church, aided and inspired by the Holy Spirit, to enable new Christians to become disciples – people who are willing and able to dedicate their lives fully to Jesus Christ,

> 'to commit themselves to all other true Christians out of love for Him, and to present their bodies to Him as a living sacrifice for all that He wants to do in His world today.'[3]

We need to gain and then maintain a balance between the experience of the Holy Spirit and being solidly rooted in God's Word. Of course, these two things should never be separated or presented as an 'either or' by the Church. However, certainly for the new Christian, it is easy for the Word and the Spirit to get out of balance. Therefore, having introduced a Seeker to Jesus Christ, and introduced that new Believer to the fullness of the Holy Spirit and encouraged them to renounce and leave behind the things that have bound them, we then need to teach our new believers the building blocks of the Christian faith. At Kingfisher, this takes the form of a seven-week Foundations course, on which, as with the Enquirers course, people are encouraged to ask any and every question. Over the seven weeks, we take people through the foundational building blocks that need to be a feature of every disciple's life: how to read the Bible and understand it; how to pray; how to get guidance; understanding and developing Christian fellowship; stewardship –

using all that we have to honour God; understanding and using your personality in evangelism; how to experience the power of the Holy Spirit in your life on an ongoing basis. This is basic teaching that will encourage the new Christian to move ahead in discipleship, rather than just start to tread water, picking up bits of information here and there.

I found out, for instance, that reading my Horoscope was a 'no no' in Christian circles six months after I became a Christian. I was attending a Bible Study group, and people were arriving a bit late, so a number of us were sitting around, waiting for the meeting to start. I spotted the host's newspaper, and so, to pass the time, I picked it up and started leafing through it. I found the horoscopes page, and was just checking mine out, as one does, when the leader of the group asked me what I was reading. When I told him, all conversation in the room stopped. Aghast faces turned to me. So, what was their problem? Maybe they wanted to know what their stars were for the day, so to ease the sudden tension, I asked the leader what his star sign was, so I could find out what was going to happen for him. It was like I had just confessed to being a mass murderer – I think a couple of them disappeared out into the back garden to start hammering a stake into the ground so I could be burned! Meanwhile, I was subjected to a lecture about how 'Christians didn't do that sort of thing.' But why not? What was the big deal, I wondered? However, not wanting to cause a scene, I quietly added that to my mental list of 'dos and don'ts' in the Christian life.

We expect new Christians to 'fit in', but we don't tell them how or why. We spend more time telling them what is wrong with their life-styles – 'You shouldn't sleep around', 'You shouldn't listen to heavy metal rock music' and so on – than we do positively explaining how they can live their lives in ways that actually do honour God, and why they need to bother to do that anyway.

There is, however, another reason for encouraging our new believers to participate in a Foundations group, and it again points to our need to start seeing things from a non-Christian perspective, rather than assuming everyone is like us. I well remember the embarrassment I felt at being lectured about reading my horoscope. I felt like I was the only one in that room that didn't know anything – I was the stupid one, and every time I opened my mouth, I got it wrong. The worst bit – remember this? – was that dreadful moment when the Bible Study leader would say, 'Let's all turn to Zephaniah, chapter two,' and there was a brief rustle of pages as everyone confidently found the passage. I used to find it **so** embarrassing to be the one who didn't even know how to **spell** Zephaniah, let alone have a clue where it was in the Bible! So, I used to go for the 'charismatic flick' – flicking through the pages, hoping against hope for a miraculous revelation of where the book of Zephaniah was. To make matters worse, week after week, well-meaning group members would draw attention to my lack of Bible knowledge by giving me helpful hints, like, 'It's just before Haggai!' Oh great! Now I have to admit that I don't know where Haggai is, either!! Nobody wants to look a fool, or stand out from the crowd in a way that highlights their lack of knowledge or understanding. In our Enquirers and Foundations groups, we make sure people have the same version of the Bible, and we tell them the page number of the passage we're looking at. We don't award Brownie points for knowing where Zephaniah is, and so no one feels stupid for not knowing. To encourage new Christians to attend a

Foundations group is to encourage them into an atmosphere where everyone knows about the same – that is, not a lot. This enables people to relax, and not feel stupid about asking the kind of questions that they assume **everyone** else already knows the answer to – like, 'Can you please explain the Trinity to me, because I seem to be having a little difficulty in fully grasping it!' I once asked my New Testament tutor at Theological College that very question, and he gave me a very wise answer: 'Join the club – I don't think I fully understand it, either!'

Disciples don't happen by accident – they need to be taught, encouraged, nurtured, challenged, forgiven, loved and, above all, planned for. If your church does not sit down and plan how it is going to encourage and enable people to be transformed into fully devoted followers of Jesus Christ, then your church will not see the emergence of disciples in its midst. Disciples are taught to obey all the commandments of God, according to Matthew 28:20. Before we write our congregations off as being wilfully disobedient sinners, unwilling to risk everything for the cause of Christ, leaders need to ask themselves, 'Have they been taught in a compelling and coherent way, on a consistent basis, what it means to be a disciple? Have I clearly articulated and demonstrated what it means to be a servant of Christ? Am I modelling full devotion to Jesus Christ in my life, and have I clearly shown from the Word of God why it is the only way for a follower of Jesus Christ to live?' To make disciples necessitates us being disciples first, and so the process of discipleship is both through learned values and taught values.

Moving from the Church of England to set up a new and independent church was, to say the least, a shock to the financial system. Despite the financial problems of the Church of England, I quickly came to appreciate that, although most Anglican clergy would consider themselves quite hard up, I had been well paid compared to the financial hardship of being supported by an independent church, where direct giving from the congregation accounts for 100% of church funds. Despite the sacrificial giving of the original team, it was (and to a certain extent, still is) very hard. Because we truly believed God had called us to reach the lost with Good News, we decided from day one not to 'pass around the offering plate' during services, because we wanted to demonstrate that people weren't just there for us to get their money – a common perception among non-Christians. We encouraged people, as they became Christians, or transferred from other churches, to prayerfully consider what they should be giving, and to give it either by Standing Order, or into the Collection Box, which was placed discreetly at the back of the church.

This has been a hard decision, but we feel that it is right before God. However, in leaving the decision about whether to give and how much to give, in the hands of each individual person, two things have become apparent. Firstly, that church goers are, in general, unaware of the biblical principles regarding giving and therefore see it as a personal favour to the church, or to the Minister, and secondly, that even when there is a right understanding of giving, people often are just not in the position to do so. It is not good enough just to turn the guilt screws on people and tell them that they are being disobedient to God by not tithing. Many people are in such a financial mess that they are just not in a position to give to God's work. As we recognised that it was neither ignorance, nor disobedience that was keeping many from giving, but rather financial mismanagement, we launched a 'financial review' service. In strict confidence, people who are drowning financially, are in debt, or who just can't seem to hold on to money, are offered the opportunity to be taken through their finances by a financial expert (yes, the Lord gave us a Bank Manager!), and shown how to formulate a sensible plan to manage their money better. People need to be helped on a practical level before they are free to respond to their desire to honour God with their lives. If people are in debt, they need to be helped to get out of debt before they can sensibly give to God's work. Disciples are **made**, they don't just happen by accident. If you want to see disciples in your church, giving sacrificially, living radically, serving in a God-honouring way, you need to develop a strategy to encourage that to happen – it won't happen on its own. We desire that our new Christians begin to eat spiritual meat, but that won't happen unless we show them how. What strategy do you have in place in your church to make disciples? Are those disciples being transformed into the likeness of Christ, free to decide for themselves to be wholly available to God, or are they being conformed into the likeness of the Minister?

Adoption in the UK is a lengthy and complicated business, as anyone will be able to verify who has been through the process. You can't just expect an Adoption Agency to give you a baby – you have to show that you have a stable home environment; that you will be trustworthy, reliable, loving, caring parents; that the child will receive the on-going support, nurture and care that it deserves. The tests are strict, the questions probing. Many aspiring couples just don't make it through the process, and those that do have a much deeper awareness of the seriousness of the undertaking than when they first applied. When we ask God to give us a heart for evangelism, so that we might reach the lost, see them come along to church, be born again and grow as Christians, it is as if we applying to His Spiritual Adoption Agency. We are asking to adopt – to become responsible for – a new spiritual baby. If an Adoption Agency is cautious and probing in its investigations, why should God be any different? He wants to know that, if He is going to entrust one of His new children into the care of a local church, that the local church in question is a place where that spiritual child is going to be loved, cared for, taught, shown what loving, healthy relationships look like, encouraged, as they grow, to play a responsible and mature part in the work of the Kingdom. If God were to ask these probing questions of your church, how do you think it might fare? Perhaps, to save embarrassment, we should ask those questions for ourselves first, before we expect the Lord to provide us with additions to the family.

Step Seven: Service

If ever I get to start a church from scratch, I thought, I'm not going to make the mistake of everyone getting over-busy. We'll have one meeting on a Sunday, one evening for Homegroups, one evening for any business meetings we need, and that's it. The rest of the time will be free for what the church should really be all about – evangelism and fellowship. Well, I have made many naive statements in my life, but this one probably takes the biscuit! It was all so simple for the first few months – pretty much like I had envisaged – but opportunities for ministry expanded rapidly ... far more rapidly than the congregation was growing. We needed to do children's work each Sunday. We needed a Book stall, a team to serve tea and coffee, a worship group, a drama group, an evangelism steering group, a team to do the PA and organise the distribution of the sermon tapes, a pastoral care team, a co-ordinator for the prayer cells, the list went on and on, and grew almost daily, as God revealed more and more of His plans for Kingfisher church. But wait a minute, Lord, haven't you forgotten something? Here You are, giving us all of these opportunities, but we're hopelessly over-stretched, with people getting more and more tired, and feeling resentful that they are being leaned upon to do things they don't want to do. The pressure to 'keep the show on the road' was becoming more and more of a headache with each passing week, especially during the time of the 'Exodus'.

This dilemma is not uncommon for small churches that have a big vision, and probably, it doesn't get a lot easier for big churches. Opportunities for ministry always seem to out-strip available resources. Consequently, church members come under pressure to work harder, give more, and receive less. This results in growing dissatisfaction with the church, frustration, guilt and a declining level of commitment. Surely there must be a better way?

During my trip to Willow Creek Community Church in February 1994, I could not help but notice that people seemed to be so motivated about what they were doing. I have already mentioned the car park attendant that I met, and there were dozens more like him. The reason for this sense of enthusiastic commitment soon became apparent. Before people sign up for service at Willow Creek, they are encouraged to take a course called Network. This course is designed to give each course member a detailed understanding of how God has 'wired them up' – what their passion is, what their Spiritual gifts are, what their temperament is. It answers not only the question, 'What should I be doing?' but 'In what area should I be doing it and how?'

I returned from Chicago feeling that God was saying something of great significance to the Church in the UK to do with Willow Creek's Network course. Having been given an initial vision of what is possible, I set about designing a similar course, shorter in length and more 'anglicised', to suit the needs of smaller, UK churches. We called this course Discovery, and now, before anyone gets involved in ministry of any kind at Kingfisher, they undergo this three-session course. We have come to realise that Discovery is not just another course, however, but a fundamental re-think of how we do church. Traditionally, the Church has come to be seen as an institution that needs to be kept running. There are jobs to be done, and we need to get people to fill those job vacancies. The question of whether those people feel called to do the job is neither here nor there – service is about taking up one's cross, dying to self and being obedient. So what if you don't like children? We **need** another leader in the children's work. Don't worry – it will only be temporary, until we find someone else (which is 'church-speak' for 'The only way out of this for you is to die, leave the church or threaten physical violence!')

However, if, instead of seeing Church as an organisation that needs to be kept going, we see it as it should be seen – as people building Community – then we start, not from the position of jobs that need to be done, but people that have been uniquely equipped by God for works of service. The goal then becomes one of enabling God's people to serve Him in the way in which He has wired them up. That may mean that we need to look again at the jobs that need to be done in Church, and break them down into their component tasks, because perhaps no one person is gifted by God to do all of the tasks associated with one job. This approach ensures that, rather than forcing pegs into holes, the holes are fashioned to fit the pegs.

When we first introduced Discovery, we had to issue a 'Government Health Warning' to our Homegroups, which was the setting for the pilot scheme. We realised that if dozens of people suddenly found that they were not serving in the way or in the place that God had designed them for, there could well be complete chaos, and so we committed to a gradual transition in the cases where people discovered that the reason why they felt failures and unfulfilled in ministry, was because they were doing the wrong thing in the wrong place and in the wrong way. We have found that, since introducing the course a year ago, people have gradually shifted into the general area of ministry that is right for them. The result? Increased motivation, a sense of doing ministry rather than just jobs, and the growth of fruitfulness and fulfilment in peoples' personal spiritual lives. Perhaps the greatest benefit of Discovery is for those with gifts of Helps, Mercy and Hospitality. Such people often feel unnoticed, un-gifted, and with nothing to offer, unlike someone with, say, a gift of healing. Discovery highlights the biblical truth that,

> *'those parts of the body that seem to be weaker are indispensable, and the parts that we think are less honourable we treat with special honour.'*
>
> (1 Corinthians 12:22–23)

No one is a reject or useless in God's eyes, and, through

Discovery, people at Kingfisher are coming to know this to be true.

The Church has often been likened to an iceberg, with twenty percent of the people doing eighty percent of the work. This is sometimes due to a lack of disciples in the church, but it is also often due to people not knowing how they can serve, or even if they can serve. People have not been taught what an honour it is to serve, and too many churches have no strategy for releasing people into fruitful service. Is there such a strategy in place in **your** church? Are ordinary, everyday Christians in your church being taught about, enthused and released into gift-based ministry, or is eighty percent of the work still being done by twenty percent of the people? The mobilisation of the laity doesn't happen by accident – it needs to form an integral part of our strategy for our church.

Step Eight: Encourage attendance at the Believers' service

One of the criticisms directed at Kingfisher, arising from our desire to reach non-Christians through our Seeker-style services, is that we only preach to people's felt needs, rather than teaching the whole counsel of God, which would include less popular subjects like holiness, righteousness and spiritual discipline. Whilst this is not true, it does point to a potential weakness in the concept of creating a church for the unchurched, while also ensuring that those already in the Kingdom are fed with more than spiritual milk. We have also been criticised for programming our Seeker services at all – how can the Spirit be free to move if there is a set programme? Underlying these criticisms is the unspoken conviction that church should be for Christians, that the services on a Sunday should minister to the needs of the already-convinced, and that, if a non-Christian should happen to be in the meeting, well, they will just naturally want to join in with what the Christians are doing. It is my conviction that this is utter selfishness on the part of Christians, and one of the major reasons that non-Christians don't tend to see the Church as being relevant, or even caring much about them.

However, we also regard as a high priority the building up and feeding of the Christians in our midst – we just don't think that you can successfully focus upon the needs of the lost and the saved at the same time. Therefore, we have designed our evening services as the time when the Believers get fed and ministered to. These are times when focus is unashamedly on God's children being in the presence of their Father, worshipping in the power of the Holy Spirit, being taught at a deeper level, and learning to minister to one another in the power of the Spirit. It is in these services that God so often touches deep and painful issues in peoples' lives, bringing out tears, laughter, long-buried pain, and speaking prophetically to us as a church as well as to individuals. These are often times of such power that people have been known to run out of the building, unable to stand the powerful presence of God. He has met with us so powerfully as we worship Him that we have been reduced to tears. There have been powerful times of silence, resting in His presence, and times of great commotion, as demons have been cast out. There have been times when non-Christians have wandered into these meetings and been struck by the power of God. Jennifer was one such person. She had recently been involved with spiritualism, was nowhere near God, but had heard about Kingfisher from someone who was a regular attendee. She came along one evening, not knowing what to expect and, as the worship started, was 'slain in the Spirit'. After she came round, she found it hard to describe what had happened, other than that she had felt an overwhelming feeling of love and warmth enveloping her and over-powering her. Jennifer has since given her life to the Lord, and is an enthusiastic member of the church.

The sermons in the Believers' services are more expository in nature, aimed both at increasing Bible knowledge, and providing direction for the church as a whole. A recent series on prayer led us into a new realm of Spiritual Warfare. As we looked more deeply into the area of binding the strongman, loosing the captives, and making godly declarations, we began to experience some major changes both in our personal lives and in the life of the church. Individuals found that attitudes at their places of work began to change. Often this brought conflict, as colleagues who had previously had no interest in spiritual things at all suddenly became hostile to Christian things and to those Christians in the office. But many fruitful conversations started popping up out of nowhere, and the church experienced further growth as a result of work colleagues being invited along.

On a church level, we began to discern in prayer the number of curses and pronouncements that had been made over the church as a whole, such as, 'Kingfisher is bound to fail, because it's not a "proper" church,' or, 'We won't allow you to join with other churches in Gloucester – you're on your own. We don't want to know you!' We began to realise just what an impact these and other curses had had on us, not just as individuals, but as a church. We felt that the church had a 'victim spirit' about it, so that we expected bad things to happen to us, and, by and large, our expectations had been proved right. We also felt like orphans, not belonging to the wider Christian community in Gloucester, because whenever we had reached out to other churches, we had been turned away. This, we realised, had resulted in an 'orphan spirit' pervading the atmosphere of the church. Both these things were stunting the growth and strangling the life out of the church, and had to be dealt with. We began standing against those attitudes, and the demonic spirits that were locking us into those patterns of behaviour, and binding them in the name of Jesus. God began to speak to us about Sonship – about our status in Him, and what, as a result, we could expect as Christians. Shortly after this, and I firmly believe as a result of this, we had a phone call from Willow Creek Community Church, asking if they could send a team of people to spend a week with us to gain experience from us! God was moving powerfully to restore us, arising from His ministry to us in the Believers' services.

The Believers' service has become the powerhouse of the church, energising and envisioning us for service in all other areas of the church. There are times when there are more bodies horizontal than vertical, though we have never sought to 'hype' times of ministry – if anything, we purposely keep them low-key. We recognise that Christians can only give what they have got, and so the building up of the believers is a high priority among us. It is so hard to find the right balance between being inward-looking and piling Christians high with an impossible load of 'oughts' and expectations. There is a phrase that has been banned in Kingfisher, which is, 'It's only church.' This phrase is a code for producing mediocre services, badly-prepared sermons, a casual attitude to holiness, surface-deep relationships and a lack of devotion to God. We seek, in our Believers' service, to enable people to catch a glimpse of the holiness, the majesty, the wonder, the awesomeness of Father God. As we gain an insight into how wonderful He truly is, how can we do anything else other than respond, *'Here am I. Send me!'* (Isaiah 6:8). The goal of our strategy is to produce disciples – fully devoted followers of Jesus Christ. That does not just happen by accident. It must be planned for, and scarce resources must be used strategically. In the light of your church's mission statement, what percentage of the activities in church are directly related to 'scoring a goal' in your church? Would you be able to review each of the activities in your church with the question, 'How is this furthering the stated mission of this church?' Are you growing disciples, or just adding to your numbers? Defining strategy is the essential key to answering these questions and ensuring that we are consistently scoring goals for the Kingdom of God.

Chapter 6

Leadership – The Make or Break Issue for the Church

Gloucester has seen many new churches start up, and whilst some of them have survived and grown, others have lasted for just a short time and then folded. I am sure that Gloucester is not unique in this, which leads us to consider the question, 'Why is it that some churches work, but others don't?' Perhaps there is an even more pertinent question, 'How can I ensure that the church I am in will survive and grow?' The answers to these questions are many and complex, but it is my belief that, at the top of the list, comes the crucial need for churches to be led by leaders. But surely by definition, the person who is designated 'Pastor' or 'Minister' is the leader of their church? They have been appointed or ordained by their denominational hierarchy, or by the consensus of the local body, and are faithfully attempting to lead that local church. However, in the Early Church, the situation was rather different. Leadership, according to Romans 12, was understood to be a spiritual gift, given to some and not to others.

I recently had a conversation with a local church leader who was experiencing disappointment and frustration in his ministry. The church of which he is the minister was not growing numerically or spiritually, there was no sense of direction or purpose among the congregation and he was disheartened. I asked him how he had come to lead this church, and he said, 'Well, we didn't have a leader, and everyone else just seemed to take a step back, leaving me to run things.' The ensuing problems and discouragements in that church were not his fault – he had been given a task for which he was not gifted. It is my belief that in the UK we have a real problem with the idea of someone having a 'gift of leadership'. We feel that, somehow, this lacks humility and is a grasping at power and authority. However, in losing the biblical understanding of leadership being a gift from God, the Church has largely come to be led by those with a Pastoral ministry, or a Teaching ministry, or an Evangelistic ministry – all of which are vital and highly esteemed giftings, but none of which is the gift that God has given to ensure the Church is well led.

Those of us that started Kingfisher had grown dissillusioned by much of what we had experienced of Church, and were asking the question, 'Why is the Church of today so different from the Early Church?' Where had the dynamic, life-changing experience of being part of a community of people who were sold out on the cause of Christ gone? We began to realise that one of the main ingredients of the Early Church was the use of spiritual gifts – people discovering how God had 'wired them up', and actually using those gifts in ministry, rather than starting with a pile of jobs that needed to be done to keep the show on the road, and then looking for 'volunteers'. We realised that, central to that philosophy of ministry in the Early Church, was the identification of those with the spiritual gift of leadership, and the release of those people into leadership roles within the church. The loss of that focus has seriously impacted the Church of today. It is vital that focus be regained, and that once again local churches are led by those with the spiritual gift of leadership. How can this gift be identified? The Bible is full of examples of godly leadership, but my favourite biblical leader is Nehemiah. At a time of national crisis, when many others would have given up, Nehemiah's gift of leadership shone through and transformed a seemingly hopeless situation into one of victory and prosperity for the Jewish people. It is very instructive to look at the characteristics that Nehemiah portrayed. They are, in essence, the characteristics that every leader will portray, and form the basis for how we identify potential leadership within our local churches.

Nehemiah had vision

We saw earlier how essential it is for a church to have a vision of what God wants it to be. However, in order for a church to have that sense of vision, it needs to be led by a person of vision. A leader has the ability to see beyond the immediate needs and problems towards a distant horizon, describe that horizon to those around them in such a way that they are inspired to head there too, and head up the expedition to get there. Nehemiah was able to cast the vision for the rebuilding of Jerusalem in an inspiring manner (Nehemiah 2:17–20) because he himself had been gripped by this vision when he had first been told about the state of the city whilst in Babylon (Nehemiah 1). As his brother Hanani recounted how the remnant were in real trouble, and how the city walls were in ruins, it was as if a 'blue touch paper' was lit within Nehemiah. His reaction to the news was that he

> *'sat down and wept. For some days I mourned and fasted and prayed before the God of heaven.'*
>
> (Nehemiah 1:4)

Often, God will implant in a leader a vision for the future, by giving him an overwhelming sense of how He views the present. Nehemiah's reaction was not just human indignation, but a sense that God's heart was breaking over the plight of His chosen people living in such disgrace in Jerusalem. A leader does not gain a sense of direction by trying to gain a consensus from the congregation. A leader will have their blue touch paper lit by God, and will feel a godly passion for 'taking the hill' that he is directing them to. This means that a leader is willing to lead the way in paying the price associated with fulfilling that vision – and there always **is** a price to pay. Calling costs – often dearly. The mark of the gifted leader is that he is willing to pay the price and not just 'talk a great story.' Nehemiah was prepared to give up his secure and comfortable job as Cupbearer to the King in order to do something about the desperate state that Jerusalem was in. This involved stepping out of his comfort zone, risking his reputation, his security, his future – even his life. But once Nehemiah's 'blue touch paper' had been lit, there was no other option for him but to pursue his calling.

Nehemiah inspired others

Though a leader has the determination to say *'Though none go with me, I still will follow'* as had Nehemiah, a further quality of a leader is the ability to inspire others with the vision that they themselves have been gripped with. This vision-casting ability produces an atmosphere of expectant faith. It motivates and inspires people to do whatever it takes to fulfil the vision. When Nehemiah said to the leaders in Jerusalem, *'Come, let us rebuild the wall of Jerusalem and we will no longer be in disgrace'* (Nehemiah 2:17), they were inspired by the idea! They replied, *'Let us start rebuilding'* (Nehemiah 2:18). But why had none of them thought of the idea for themselves? Because the spiritual gift of leadership is about looking beyond what we have now, to a preferred future. Today, far too many churches accept the position that the current situation of the church cannot change. We are locked into small, weak, inward-looking congregations which are largely ignored by our local communities, and we don't see how that can possibly change. Which is why there is such a desperate need for the spiritual gift of leadership to be rediscovered and released into the local and national Church. Leaders inspire people with a God-given vision of what things could be like. Leaders motivate people to great acts of heroism and selflessness.

Another great leader in the Bible, despite his personal problems, was King David. Because he displayed the spiritual gift of leadership, people around were prepared to rise to great hights of heroism – as in, for instance, the episode recounted in 2 Samuel 23.

> *'During harvest time, three of the thirty chief men came down to David at the cave of Adullam, while a band of Philistines was encamped in the valley of Rephaim. At that time, David was in the stronghold, and the Philistine garrison was at Bethlehem. David longed for water and said, "Oh that someone would*

> *give me a drink of water from the well near the gate of Bethlehem!" So the three mighty men broke through the Philistine lines, drew water from the well near the gate of Bethlehem and carried it back to David. But he refused to drink it; instead he poured it out before the Lord. "Far be it from me, O Lord, to do this!" he said. "Is it not the blood of men who went at the risk of their lives?" And David would not drink it.'*
>
> (2 Samuel 23:13–18)

What an astonishing act of heroism! But this was the atmosphere that had been created by the spiritual gift of leadership in operation in David's life. Leaders not only have vision – they have the ability to cast that vision in such a compelling way that ordinary, everyday people are fired with a burning passion to do whatever it takes to 'take the hill' that their leader is pointing to. Sadly, this ability to cast a vision is often used to manipulate or abuse others. A leader who is not under accountability is truly dangerous! However, when the leader is submitted to God and the accountability of other mature Christians, and their gift is submitted to the goal of glorifying God, a group of refugees can become an army, and a pile of rubble, the scorn of the neighbours, can become an impregnable city, as Nehemiah demonstrates.

Nehemiah knew how to delegate

One of the major barriers to growth in the Church today is a lack of understanding of the need to draw together teams of people to accomplish the vision. There is a great expectation placed on full-time clergy to provide the primary pastoral care in the church, chair all the meetings, be the resident caretaker, represent the church in the community and so on. If the Vicar, or Pastor has not called to see you, then the church does not care about you. Faced with these sorts of expectations, the thought of the church growing will leave many exhausted and demoralised ministers feeling dismayed. How will they possibly cope with yet more people, yet more demands on their time? However, a person with the spiritual gift of leadership will both understand and agree with a comment made by Carl George, on the subject of breaking church growth barriers:

> 'In short, I suggest a changed paradigm for church leadership. You must shift from doing the caring, which usually means you do it yourself, to seeing to it that people get cared for, which means that you develop and manage a system of care giving that will include as many of your church's lay leaders as possible.'[1]

He suggests that the leader who is leading their church to growth will be making the switch from the doing of 'hands-on' ministry to the creating of an infrastructure where the laity is mobilised in a strategic way to do the 'hands-on' ministry themselves.

Let's look at how Nehemiah set about doing this. Chapter 3 describes Nehemiah's strategy. He had done a survey of the perimeter of the city and had divided it up into sections. He had then given each of those sections to different people, and made them responsible for the rebuilding of their particular section. Nehemiah, meanwhile, maintained an overview of the entire project, in order to not only oversee the building work, but to be free to respond to the fresh challenges that came from their disgruntled neighbours. He didn't allow himself to be drawn away from his primary role of oversight and into one particular, specialised area of the rebuilding project. Many leaders today make the valiant attempt to delegate the various areas of ministry in their church, only to be dragged into another area of ministry. Leaders need to lead, though, and are only free to do so effectively if their time and energy is not taken up in doing 'hands on' ministry. Because Nehemiah had the spiritual gift of leadership, he had the ability to plan strategically, to identify and train those whom God was equipping to fulfil the various parts of the plan, and to release them into ministry, thus freeing himself for his God-given role of oversight and future planning. To maintain that position of not being dragged back into providing primary care (or of not running voluntarily back into it!) takes courage, commitment and vision-casting, ensuring that the congregation understands and is inspired by a vision of what could be achieved if the leader is only free to lead.

Nehemiah established core values

The situation that began to develop in Jerusalem is one that is similar to many growing churches today. The former pile of rubble was being transformed into something that was causing passers-by to stop and take note. People were beginning to believe in the possibility of the vision becoming a reality. A reputation for being a radical, exciting, go-ahead place was beginning to be established. And yet, just below the surface, some serious problems were beginning to come to light. Chapter 5 describes the growing sense of discontent among the rank-and-file Jews concerning the social and economic hardships being felt, and particularly at the exploitation of the poor by the rich. However, these black clouds were largely hidden from public view and so far as the general public were concerned, Jerusalem under Nehemiah was a success story. Sooner or later, the leader of any growing church is faced with the dilemma of having to choose between reputation and character – keeping the show on the road, so that the 'success story' continues, or confronting what is really going on at the risk of ruining their reputation. The character of the leader is laid bare at times like these, and although there is an almost overwhelming desire not to rock a successful boat, the overheads of not tackling difficult internal issues in order to build character will eventually be found to be very high indeed.

Nehemiah was a great leader, because he recognised that there was little point in rebuilding the wall of Jerusalem, if the character of the Jewish people was rotten. Nehemiah did, therefore, what all those with the spiritual gift of leadership are called to do – he established core values, and ensured that those values were adhered to. The establishment of core values is the difference between the seed that fell on the shallow soil which sprang up rapidly but whose growth was not sustainable, and the seed that fell on the good soil, put down roots and enjoyed steady, sustainable growth. A wise leader will be far more concerned with establishing the values that will carry the church into the future – values that are going to build long-term character that will sustain the church in the hard times and ensure that the church remains on track – than with attempting to build a great reputation through fantastic growth, great programmes, or a high-profile ministry. This does not have to be a navel-gazing exercise, where the church becomes self-absorbed and inward-looking. However, the church will lack focus, be unable to develop strategy and will, ultimately go nowhere, if it has not clearly defined those values it holds dear: values such as building relationships that are God-honouring; telling the truth and pursuing honesty and reality; giving priority to the lost; pursuing lives that are wholly devoted to Christ, and so on. As you reflect upon your church, can you pinpoint what the core values are? Have they been clearly articulated, or are they just something that people tend to stumble across as they get more involved in the church? Are they the values that are really in practice in the church, or, in reality, is there another set of values in place? Who put them in place? Perhaps you should pause for a moment and try to clarify just what those core values really are.

Nehemiah could identify strengths and weaknesses in people and organisations

Leaders tend to be pro-active, rather than reactive. That is to say, they act to head off potential problems before they become actual crises. They recognise the weakness of the dictum, 'If it isn't broken, don't fix it', recognising that, on the surface it may look fine, but trouble is brewing for the future, and so let's take action to fix it now, before it actually falls apart causing upset and distress. On the more positive side, a leader can spot positive potential in people and organisations that would pass others by, and can begin a process of bringing that potential to fruition. We have already seen how this worked in Nehemiah's situation in terms of him looking beneath the apparent success of the building project to the cracks that had appeared in the social fabric of the community. However, on the positive side, look at how the building project got started in the first place. Suddenly, as is described in Chapter 3, there was an abundance of skilled labourers, all willing and able to help rebuild the wall! Where did they all come from? Prior to Nehemiah's return, nobody seemed capable of doing anything, but all of a sudden, there was a large, committed workforce. Nehemiah, using his spiritual gift of leadership, was able to motivate and organise people to use gifts and skills they never knew they had. Motivation is the key word. It turns defeated, demoralised, seemingly un-gifted people into energetic, talented, gifted servants of God. The major problem for the Jews living in the rubble of Jerusalem was not that they didn't have the skills or the knowledge of how to rebuild – they lacked the motivation and the vision.

Nehemiah didn't bring in skilled labourers from Babylon to carry out the work – he spotted the potential from among the Home Team, motivated them with the vision, organised them, equipped them and released them into action. Leaders spot potential, both positive and negative, and act upon it in a pro-active way, rather than waiting for the organisation to grind to a halt, or for the opportunity to pass by. The situation in Jerusalem before Nehemiah arrived is remarkably similar to the situation in many local churches today. We lack numbers and finances, we are marginalised and ignored in our communities, the needs seem so overwhelming, and we seem so few and so ineffective. To someone with the spiritual gift of leadership, though, this isn't a hopeless and demoralising situation at all. It is pregnant with possibilities, and the key is motivating and envisioning the people, however few there are, spotting their potential, encouraging their strengths, casting vision, and challenging the accepted notion that it is inevitable that we will go on eking out a living among this pile of rubble forever.

As you think through the members of your congregation, what impression do you get? A sense of despondency at the poor hand that God has dealt you? Or a sense of excitement at the untapped potential within each person? The answer to that question goes a long way to answering the other question, 'Do I have the spiritual gift of leadership, or not?'

Nehemiah encouraged and released other leaders

Nehemiah had had a pretty rough time in seeking to fulfil his calling to rebuild Jerusalem. He had been intimidated, slandered, discouraged, attacked ... but he persevered and won through in the end. Chapter 6 records how, finally, the wall was completed (6:15ff). He would have been forgiven for feeling justified in sitting back and enjoying the fruit of his labour. He had beaten off the opposition, everyone agreed on who was boss, things were finally going Nehemiah's way. So what did he do? He handed over the leadership of Jerusalem to his brother, Hanani! Why on earth would Nehemiah want to hand over the leadership reins, just when everything was beginning to go so well? Because the person with the spiritual gift of leadership delights in encouraging and releasing others who have that same gift of leadership. They create a culture whereby leaders and potential leaders start appearing. Leaders attract leaders, and rejoice in equipping and releasing leaders. They rejoice in the emergence of other leaders, rather than feel threatened by them. A leader will not feel secure if their church cannot function without them – he or she will feel uneasy, because this is not a healthy situation. A leader delights in doing himself out of a job, because another leader who has been trained, equipped and released has taken over those responsibilities. However, there is a great temptation to create a leadership culture where budding leaders are moulded into the shape and style of the senior leader in the church, rather than finding and developing their own style.

Nehemiah appointed Hanani (7:2) not because they were brothers, nor because Hanani was a clone of Nehemiah's style, but for two crucial reasons: he was a man of integrity, and he feared God more than most men do. These, it seems to me, are two crucial features to be looked for in those who would become leaders. Have you ever wondered what they word 'integrity' means? It comes from the word 'integer', which means 'whole number', rather than a fraction. In other words, having a heart of integrity means having a heart that is not divided – it is being wholehearted. Another word closely related to integrity is the word 'integrated'; everything working together in harmony. This is God's desire for all His people, but particularly for those He has called into leadership. As Lee Strobel has put it:

> 'Integrity means a wholeness or integration between your **beliefs** and **behaviour**, between your **creed** and **character**, between your **faith** and your **formulation of policies**.'[2]

Nehemiah spotted integrity – wholeness – in his brother, Hanani. He had a 'what you see is what you get' quality about him that is vital for any leader, but particularly so for a Christian leader.

Is there a leadership culture in your church? Such an atmosphere is vital if the church is to grow. However, although the presence of someone with the spiritual gift of leadership leading the church encourages others with the same gift to be identified, leaders do not grow and mature by chance. The church is one of the only organisations I know that consistently puts people into positions of responsibility and authority without providing adequate – or any – training. How many of our Small Group leaders have been given instruction in the workings of group dynamics? Do we train our Elders, our PCC members or our Leadership Teams in how to motivate others, how to delegate, how to develop and disciple others? Sadly, all too often, the answer to these questions is 'No'. To encourage new leadership to develop in the Church, we need to develop training programmes. Without in-house training, the usual scenario seems to be that the senior leadership positions are inevitably filled by people imported from elsewhere. How many of the senior positions in your church are filled by people who have come to Christ in your church, have matured under the teaching in your church, have had their spiritual gifts identified and affirmed by the leadership of your church and are now themselves ministering in a leadership position in your church? Those with the spiritual gift of leadership need to see it as their priority to invest their time and energy in motivating, training and equipping home-grown talent – people with local credibility, who are demonstrating a commitment to being disciples, and who are beginning to manifest the spiritual gift of leadership.

At Kingfisher, we have tried to be intentional about this, rather than just leaving it to chance. Leaders and apprentice leaders are taught the theory of leadership at leaders' group meetings, are given the opportunity to put that theory into practice in group situations and are formally reviewed. Actually, everything that is done at Kingfisher is reviewed, in order that we learn to use better the gifts that God has given us. Small Group leaders, for example, are trained in group dynamics, are encouraged to formulate aims and objectives for their group which will then be reviewed periodically by an Elder, and are encouraged to examine ruthlessly the reasons for their groups not working out as well as they should be. Because an essential aspect of one who has a gift of leadership is a servant heart, leaders welcome rather than resent this kind of input. The Lord deserves the very best that we have, and so do His people, so there is no room for empire building or being territorial – we need to be consistently maturing, developing and becoming more effective in ministry. Putting in place a formal review procedure, far from being unspiritual or 'heavy', provides the right mechanism for encouraging growth in people, particularly leaders. It also takes the confrontation out of encouraging people to change and improve.

Nehemiah understood that the nature of leadership is servanthood

Being Governor of Jerusalem must have been a great position. Backed up by the might of the Babylonian Empire, yet far enough away to run things the way you want to without too much interference, the people you govern beaten and bowed into submission with no choice but to do what you tell them: the temptation to become a corrupt dictator must have been powerful indeed. Yet we read in Nehemiah 5:14–15:

> *'Moreover, from the twentieth year of King Artaxerxes, when I was appointed to be their governor in the*

> *land of Judah, until his thirty-second year – twelve years – neither I nor my brothers ate the food allotted to the governor. But the earlier governors – those preceding me – placed a heavy burden on the people and took forty shekels of silver for them in addition to food and wine. Their assistants also lorded it over the people. But out of reverence for God, I did not act like that.'*

This is such a crucial aspect of leadership and yet one so often overlooked. Ask around your church what the word 'leadership' means to people, and you will probably get many replies – but one you probably won't get is the word 'servanthood'. Which is reasonable enough, because it seems universally true in the market place that the strong survive and succeed, whereas caring, sharing and putting others first is for losers. The recent massive recession felt all around the world and particularly in the UK has heightened this. It's not just a question of getting ahead in your career now – if you want to survive at all, you need to out-pace the rivals who used to be your workmates. Any promotion that is still out there is fought over less subtly and more viciously that ever before. You can't afford to be a loser. Nice people don't succeed – you have to be prepared to 'do whatever it takes' to get on in life.

This isn't a new message – for as long as there have been people there has been the desire to succeed. But how do we know that we have succeeded? By measuring our success against other people. If you're not convinced of this, remember back to the last time you received a pay rise at work. If it was a good one, you probably felt elation and a sense of achievement, as well as excitement at the thought of having some extra money. But what would have been your reaction if, two minutes after those emotions burst upon you, you discovered that your work-mates had all received a pay rise as well, except that theirs was double what you got! Still feeling elated? No way! You feel cheated, angry ... a failure. Why did they get more than me? I'm better than they are. I'm worth more than they are. These are basic human reactions – reactions that are by no means new, and Christians are by no means immune from them. Remember one particularly sticky moment between Jesus' disciples when they felt their positions were under threat? Matthew 20:20–28 tells the story of the mother of Zebedee's sons trying to do a deal with Jesus to secure for him a leadership position in heaven. When the other disciples heard about this they were outraged. Their outrage, though, stemmed not from a sense of how forward and presumptuous these two disciples were being, but from a feeling of losing ground, of falling behind in the race to be top dog. Jesus' response to this cuts to the heart of the matter, demonstrating the key difference between someone who aspires to rule over people, and someone who has the spiritual gift of leadership.

> *'You know that the rulers of the Gentiles lord it over them, and their high officials exercise authority over them. Not so with you. Instead, whoever wants to become great among you must be your servant, and whoever wants to be first must be your slave – just as the Son of Man did not come to be served but to serve, and to give his life as a ransom for many.'*
>
> (Matthew 20:25–28)

Nehemiah, centuries earlier, had grasped this truth. He could have 'lorded it over' the residents of Jerusalem, but he didn't. Why? Out of reverence for God (Nehemiah 5:15). His desire (which should be matched by our desire) was to revere God – to exalt and magnify Him – in what he did, which is basic to having a servant heart. This highlights motivation in leadership. Nehemiah's motivation was God's honour and glory.

But many leaders are motivated by rather different things, such as reputation, the need for recognition amongst their peers, the fear of failure and so on. If our utmost desire is to bring glory to God, and our next desire is for the well-being and discipleship of our congregations, then God is able to use our spiritual gift of leadership in a powerful and effective way. The overheads of having wrong motives when exercising the gift of leadership are enormous. The phenomenon of Spiritual Abuse has only recently begun to be recognised as being as widespread as it is. In fact, Spiritual Abuse is rampant in Church life today. Every bit as destructive as physical abuse, a victim of Spiritual Abuse is made to feel worthless, incapable of surviving in a relationship with God on their own, a failure, and, very often, will want nothing more to do with the Church. Spiritual Abuse happens when the leadership of a church seek to 'lord it over' their congregation, rather than seeing it as a privilege to serve. As already indicated throughout this book, Kingfisher exists to reach lost people – but there are many people who are lost, though they are already saved. They have lost their way, like Sue, in the introduction to this book, because, in their wounded state they were abused by the Church, made to feel worthless and, somehow, 'at fault'. For many such people, coming to Kingfisher has been the start of the process of recovery – learning to forgive, to *'be transformed by the renewing of their minds'*, to take heart in the overwhelming, unconditional love of God. Many have come to see that they are not failures because they didn't live up to past Christian leaders' expectations, but rather were victims of abuse.

However, we have sadly seen how others, having come out of abusive situations and spent a while in the healing atmosphere of Kingfisher, have opted to return to the same (or an even worse) abusive environment. Why would they willingly do this? Well that, as the title to David Johnson and Jeff VanVonderen's excellent book highlights, is 'The Subtle Power of Spiritual Abuse.'[3] Spiritual Abuse creates a dependency culture which, without ministry to be set free from it, will reassert itself sooner or later. A person who has been abused in this way will not find freedom merely through changing church, or even moving to a new area. We have observed that, when people are abused in this way, it creates a spiritual bondage that manifests itself either in suspicion or rebellion towards subsequent leaders who may be godly people, or a desire to find the imagined safety of another, similarly abusive leader. Whilst the phenomenon of Spiritual Abuse is only now receiving the attention that it merits, it has been rife in the Church for many years. There is, as highlighted by Nehemiah, a great difference between strong and abusive leadership, and that difference is seen primarily in the attitude of humility in that leader (or lack of it). Here, taken from a talk given by Clive Corfield are some of the characteristics of a leader who is walking in humility:

- They love to serve others and don't feel threatened by others' success
- They seek forgiveness and reconciliation
- They don't judge people and they aren't critical, though they **are** discerning

- They are willing to accept correction through their desire to grow more like Jesus
- They long for others to be blessed and honestly rejoice with them when that happens
- They are generous and seek to release others into all that God has for them
- Their focus is upon God's kingdom and God's honour, rather than their own
- They don't run themselves down through false humility, but they **do** make sure that God gets the credit

Here, on the other hand, are some characteristics of a leader who is ministering out of an attitude of pride:

- They talk in terms of 'My gifting' or 'My ministry' and recite stories that show themselves in a flattering light
- They demand to be treated in a manner that befits their status as leader, insisting on their rights and privileges
- They are insecure about other peoples' giftings, especially those with the gift of leadership
- They become very defensive when challenged, and find it hard to accept correction
- They tend to take credit for what God as done, especially when talking to other ministers
- They compare their performance with other people, tending to run down other ministries
- They find it hard to tell the truth about the ministry they are involved in, especially when someone asks them how big their church is! (Note: my good friend, Clive Corfield says that he always answers that question by saying, 'Oh, between 3 and 5000!' which should, or course, cover just about every church in the UK!)

- They tend to pursue reputation rather than character
- They tend to be impatient with those around them, finding that criticism comes easier than praise[4]

This last list isn't intended to be used to point the finger at any particular leader that we might know, but it does look pretty familiar, doesn't it? The Church today is in desperate need of strong leadership, but instead it is riddled with abusive leadership, where strength is measured in terms of domination, manipulation and control. The book of Nehemiah speaks prophetically to today's Church – not only in the area of rebuilding the ruins, but in giving insight into how the authentic gift of leadership is worked out in practice. It has been our experience at Kingfisher that the key to effective leadership is the character of the individual – the willingness to serve sacrificially, lay down one's life for the cause of Christ, and walk in humility. Without these characteristics, anyone exercising a position of leadership is, indeed, a dangerous person, and will affect the spiritual life of the entire group of people they are leading. Even a cursory glance at the books of 2 Kings and Chronicles confirms this. However, on the other side of that coin, when the authentic gift of leadership is recognised, nurtured and released into the Body of Christ, tremendous things happen. An atmosphere of faith is born. Vision is cast. People discover gifts and ministries they never even dreamed of. The Church grows qualitatively and quantitatively. So, pray for your leaders. Pray for the spiritual gift of leadership to be loosed in your church – and, having lit the blue touch paper, enjoy the fireworks!

Evaluation points

- If you are in a position of leadership in your local church, which of the leadership characteristics of

Nehemiah, highlighted above, can you identify with? Which of them do you perceive as being weak points for you?

- Do you find yourself identifying more strongly with the leader who operates out of humility, or the leaders who operates out of pride? Do you find yourself excited by, or threatened by, those with emerging leadership gifts?
- What steps do you propose to take, in order that an increasing number of leaders are identified, trained and released in your church?

Chapter 7

Small Groups – Growing Big by Staying Small

It was all going to be so simple. If I ever started a church from scratch, I thought, I would keep it simple – give people enough time to get to know each other . . . develop friendships and fellowship. I would keep meetings to the absolute minimum – you shouldn't need more than the Sunday services, a mid-week prayer meeting and an occasional business meeting. Anything more than that and we're getting bogged down in unnecessary trivia. As I've already mentioned, it all seemed so simple then! Of course, as anyone in church leadership knows, things never work out as straightforwardly as that. Before long there were groups for music, drama, pastoral care, finance, children's work; in fact, we began to think that God had made a serious mistake in only allocating seven evenings per week. Didn't He realise we needed at least ten? Added to all of this busyness was a steady stream of new people coming into the church, many of them seekers wanting to know more about the Christian faith. It wasn't long before the early sense of togetherness and mutual commitment that we had felt as a new fellowship began to evaporate. All of a sudden, people began to feel disconnected from one another – the quality of care being experienced within the church began to deteriorate, as things got busier and busier. It wasn't that people cared less, but rather than they were just too busy, and feeling swamped by new faces appearing each week. And as fast as those faces were appearing, they seemed to be disappearing because they weren't experiencing the kind of personal care they needed and expected.

The above scenario is a problem common to many growing churches today, and one of the major reasons that the growth of a church plateaus around the 75–150 person mark. Inadequate care, over-stressed clergy, lack of quality discipleship all add up to limitation on growth. In the midst of all of this busyness, the thought of committing oneself to a house group or Bible study group is one of those 'I know I ought to, but I just haven't got the energy or the time' scenarios. Who needs yet another commitment? And yet, there is a growing realisation among Church Growth analysts that the Small Group is the very tool God is giving us to cope with growth and the busyness and change that comes with it. The church that will consistently grow and meet the needs of its growing population, is the church that is able to provide quality care and attention to each member of the church in a way that is not adversely affected by growth in numbers or proliferation of ministry within the church.

As Carl George rightly observes:

> 'For this to happen, self-help caring must be developed as a mutual resource throughout a churchwide system of lay-led Small Groups.'[1]

Rather than seeing Small Groups as yet more calls on our

already-overstretched time, the Small Group becomes the place where, amidst all the change and growth around me, I find a group of people who are committed to me, whom I can rely upon, and whom I am growing in conjunction with. The Small Groups become the building blocks of the church, and they unlock unlimited growth potential in the church. This way of looking at church has become known as Meta-Church, from the Greek word *meta*, denoting change. A church organised around a network of Small Groups has the flexibility to continually grow and, therefore, change. No matter how big a church grows, if it is organised around the building blocks of Small Groups, it will be able to minister to hurting people to a consistent standard, because the care of those people is in the hands of an increasing number of trained lay people, responsible for just the eight to twelve people in their group. Of course, the concept of cell, congregation and celebration is not a new one. However, it is my belief that the potential of the cell has been consistently under-realised, with the focus of pastoral care still being centred on a few specialists trying to care for people at the congregation level. Inevitably as the congregation grows, the quality of care goes down. Meta-church stresses that pastoral care should primarily happen in the Small Group, be it a Bible study group, a specialist group such as a worship group, or an affinity-based group such as a New Mums' group. The immediate stumbling block to this approach to church is the lack of leaders. If everyone is to be cared for primarily in the Small Group that they attend, which releases one of the major limiters to growth, there is a constant demand for new leaders, which always seems to outstrip supply.

Rather than this being a discouragement to focusing on Small Groups as a means of growth, this highlights once again the crucial need both of vision and strategy. If our vision is to grow both numerically and in terms of discipleship, then our strategy must be to identify and develop the spiritual gift of leadership. Having had our Discovery course in operation for two years now, we have been able to identify a large number of people whom God is gifting with leadership potential. Small Group leaders are given training in how to apprentice these potential leaders, giving them exposure to Small Group leadership in a safe setting, feeding back on their performance, offering helpful pointers for next time. We aim to be pro-active in training leaders – that is to say, we don't wait for the crisis of a new group with no-one to lead it, but rather we are continually training potential leaders in order to release them into Small Group leadership when a group is ready to be formed. A crucial role becomes that of overseeing the small group structure of the church – a leader with the sole responsibility of training, equipping and releasing Small Group leadership, and providing on-going training and accountability.

I said earlier that for all the familiarity regarding cell, congregation, and celebration structures, the cell level has been consistently under-utilised, even under-valued. You may feel that this is an unfair comment ... that the house groups in your church have been working well for years. However, for most churches, the critical event in their calendar is the Sunday service. The focus, in terms of time, effort and expenditure lies in the preparation of the sermon, the worship and the fellowship before and after the service. The critical event in the Meta-Church model, however, is the meeting together of the Small Group. This is where I am primarily cared for. This is where I learn to practise my spiritual gifts, where I pursue discipleship, where I discover accountability, where I risk vulnerability. Is the Sunday service no longer of importance? Of course it is, but it no longer labours under the impossible burden of being all things to all people – a charismatic knees-up; a place of in-depth teaching; a place of individual attention; an opportunity for in-depth counselling; a place to bring my non-Christian friend – all at the same time. It makes possible the desire to be more focused in the main service, because the quite legitimate needs of the church members – and those who are still seeking – are being met by the critical event of the church – the Small Group. The quality of the Sunday services will increase, too, because the care of the congregation, however large it becomes, is primarily met by any one of the ever-expanding number of Small Group leaders. This frees the minister and the senior leadership from that which is not their primary calling to that which is – the oversight of the church, the attention to prayer and the ministry of the word. This is the conclusion the Twelve arrived at in Acts 6, which resulted in the appointing of Deacons. The delegating of primary care to the Small Group level will have the same freeing results for us today.

In addition to identifying and releasing those with the spiritual gift of leadership, there are two other hurdles to be overcome before Meta-Church can become a reality in your church. The first is the re-orientation of the congregation, so that they are looking to their Small Group leader for pastoral care (and indeed, so that they are actually **in** a Small Group in the first place!) and, perhaps most crucially, the re-orientation of the minister. This entails a shift from doing the caring oneself, to seeing to it that people get cared for, through focusing more on the big picture, equipping and releasing those who are going to be doing the primary care and resisting the temptation to slip back into primary care-giving. This is more easily said than done, for a number of reasons.

Firstly, most full-time ministers were taught that a good minister visits old ladies (and men!), comforts the sick and dying in hospital, is on call whenever for whoever, preaches twice a week or more and runs all the major committees in the church. Secondly, it is difficult to measure productivity as a minister, so most ministers have a sneaking suspicion that their congregation feel they aren't pulling their weight. This is especially acute if the minister is paid directly by the congregation. Therefore, the busier the minister looks and the more time he spends on tangible things like visiting, running meetings, etc., the less guilty and judged he or she feels. It's so difficult to answer the question, 'So, what **do** you do during the week, then?' that there is a familiar stab of guilt and a feeling of inadequacy constantly lurking whenever that question is asked. Often, ministers are manipulated into feeling guilty about delegating work to lay people, because they already have 'proper' jobs, and are already hard-pressed, without the full-time, paid minister off-loading his or her own job onto them.

Consequently, it is by no means an easy shift to make, from that of being the primary care-giver to that of being the enabler of other primary care-givers. However, it is the crucial paradigm shift, if the quality of care is to remain constant whilst the church grows and diversifies. David Yonggi Cho, Pastor of the world's largest church, tells how he worked himself to exhaustion leading his church. Eventually he collapsed under the strain and was hospitalised. As his staff gathered around his hospital bed, he instructed them to take over the leadership of the church in his absence. At first, they were reluctant, because who could step into the great man's shoes?

However, as is so often the case, necessity became the mother of invention, and this brought Yoido Full Gospel church's cell system came into being. Today there are in excess of 55,000 trained cell group leaders. A wonderful success story? Undoubtedly, but brought about only through the collapse of the Pastor's health, bringing about the crisis which forced him into a more realistic mode of ministry – the realisation that however much he loved his congregation and however much he desired to care for them all, he just couldn't do it on his own.

Insecurity, guilt, bad training and low self-esteem cause many ministers to fail to release the pastoral care and discipleship of their congregations into the hands of lay leadership, and are, therefore, too busy and tired to identify, train and release that lay leadership, which becomes a vicious circle. Breaking out of that circle is crucial, and is brought about through leaders and congregation together gaining a biblical understanding of the priesthood of all believers, and together having a passion for adequately caring for the sheep that God is giving them. Leaders need support and encouragement in breaking the guilt and insecurity cycle if the church is ever to be released into the unlimited growth that God wants for it, and at the same time experience quality, consistent care.

Necessity, so often, really is the mother of invention. In recent times, the Lord has been opening up for me greater opportunities to travel and speak internationally. There are an ever-increasing number of churches joining the Kingfisher Association of Churches, and a growing number of conferences and seminars to be organised and taught. I have given up the idea that I am the most effective person, or even the most gifted person to provide care for people, and this has enabled a re-organisation of the church along the lines of Exodus 18, with Elders overseeing different areas of ministry, each area of ministry comprising various Small Groups. Consequently, the church is free from the bottleneck of my lack of availability, and everyone has the opportunity to be in a meaningful relationship with a Small Group of people, cared for by a Small Group leader who is focusing on the pastoral care and spiritual development of their Small Group. Or, at least, that is the theory!

Actually, there are constant temptations and subtle pressures to get back to providing the primary care. Training and overseeing leaders is often more frustrating and less satisfying than actually doing the job oneself. Being honest, I often don't need manipulating very hard to fall back into trying to be omnipresent and omnicompetent, even though I know both are beyond my reach. My guess is that I am not alone in this struggle, and that many leaders struggle with a sense of guilt and even failure at not being there for everyone all the time. And yet, if we truly love those God has placed in our care, we will ensure that they are well cared for on a consistent basis, despite the feelings of insecurity that brings to us leaders. Small Groups really are the only way to provide that care without limiting the growth potential of your church.

Evaluation points

- If you had a sensitive problem, who would you talk it through with in the church? Would that person be available to provide on-going support, care and accountability?
- If the church that you go to were to double in size over the next month, how would the level and quality of pastoral care be affected?

- Do you know everyone in your church? If not, does this worry you?
- What are your expectations regarding the Small Group that you are in? Is it one more commitment that you could do without, or is it meeting real needs in your life? In what ways would you change the group that you are in?

Chapter 8

Mobilising the Whole Church for Spiritual Warfare

Recently, I was on a speaking tour in Malawi. I was there to teach at various churches, and to welcome six churches in particular into the Kingfisher Association of Churches. Each of these churches was in a remote, rural area of the country, and so I spent hours each day bumping along pot-holed roads in a beaten-up taxi, wondering if this is what Reinhardt Bonkke has to put up with in order to fulfil his ministry in Africa!

One of the churches I visited early on in the trip was in a village a couple of hours outside Blantyre in Southern Malawi. When I arrived at the village, I immediately sensed a depressed, almost mournful atmosphere about the place. The church gradually filled up, and a time of praise started, which really struggled. During this time, a woman stood up and started haranguing the crowd. All my interpreter would say by way of a translation was, 'She says, "We must be free!"' I did my talk which went down like a lead balloon, and afterwards I waited around in the village square as the Pastor went to visit the sick people. There were many people who had malaria, and several were dying. It just seemed to reinforce the sense of doom and gloom in the village, which added to my feelings of depression after my talk had gone so badly.

That evening, as I was praying in my hotel room, that woman's words came back to me, and the Lord impressed upon me that they were prophetic words. 'We must be free!' Free from what? As I prayed further about this, the Lord revealed to me that the whole village was under the influence of an area, or territorial, spirit of death. That death was being manifest in both the physical and spiritual realm. I felt very stirred up to pray about this, and for the next few hours, I engaged in Spiritual Warfare on behalf of that village, binding the spirits of death and fear, taking authority in the name of Jesus and declaring an end to their reign of terror in that place, rebuking the powers of darkness that would seek to keep God's people separated from all that He has promised them. Then I prayed that a spirit of joy, of life and of worship would be loosed on that village.

I was able, right at the end of my stay in Malawi, to go back to that same village. As we approached (in the even more beaten-up taxi), I couldn't help but wonder whether the warfare that I had waged that night would have had any real effect. Would I be able to notice any real difference, or was it all just in the mind? I was soon to get my answer. As we arrived in the village square, we heard the sound of singing coming from the church. Going into the church, we found the place packed, and I was completely overwhelmed by the almost physical presence of God. I don't normally swing from the chandeliers, but I could feel tears welling up in my eyes as I felt surrounded by the presence of the Lord in a way that I have seldom, if ever felt before. After the praise died down, it was time for me to speak. The response was terrific, with the congregation breaking into spontaneous praise to God in the middle of it. At the end, the Pastor announced that I was about to leave, so they were going to pray for me. Suddenly, there was an outburst of intercessory prayer from the congregation, which turned to an amazing time of warfare prayer. What an incredible difference! It taught me a valuable lesson about the reality of Spiritual Warfare, and has planted in me a renewed passion to see the Church equipped in this area. Indeed, any church that has a stated desire to reach lost people had better also be taking Spiritual Warfare seriously, because, in the words of Reinhardt Bonkke, we are populating heaven by plundering hell, which plunges us immediately into the arena of direct conflict with Satan.

There commonly seem to be two errors that people fall into when approaching this subject – to ascribe everything to Satan, or to dismiss the whole idea as being the product of the imagination of the lunatic fringe. Both of these views are, or course, defective. Satan is alive, active and organised, but he often doesn't need to get involved – we do a very good job of sinning all on our own! In order to get a balanced position and, therefore, to mobilise the whole church – not just the Spiritual Warfare sub-committee – a strategy must be developed and put in place to equip and release ordinary Christians into this realm. As J. John, the evangelist, once put it, so many things the Church says we ought to do leaves him responding with: YBH ... Yes, But How?! We rarely teach our new Christians to pray ordinary everyday prayers, let alone how to sensibly and safely engage in warfare in such a way that they also remain relevant to the real world, able to witness in a sane and rational way to their non-Christian friends. How do we go about bringing the reality of the spiritual battle into the life of the church and mobilise people to pray accordingly, recognising the seriousness of it, but not appearing as raving charismaniacs to those they are trying to attract into the Kingdom of God? We have found the following to be effective, and have found that, as Spiritual Warfare comes to be seen as the norm in the Christian life, captives are set free, disciples are made and the Kingdom of God advances in exciting ways.

Keep a correct focus

The goal of Spiritual Warfare is not to defeat Satan. The defeat of Satan was accomplished on the cross, and that was the decisive victory. Indeed, I believe that one of the enemy's more subtle tactics is to divert as much energy and attention away from the true mission of the Church – to win lost souls for Christ and to present a spotless bride to the coming Bridegroom – by encouraging a lot of time-consuming and energy-sapping sabre-rattling from the Church. It is, of course, true that Satan and his legions are still alive and active in the world, but they **have been** defeated already, though they continuously need reminding of that fact!

What, then, is the goal of Spiritual Warfare, if not to defeat an already defeated adversary? The goal is to become Christ-like, so that we may be presented *'as a pure virgin to him'* (2 Corinthians 11:2). Our focus, then, is not Satan, but Christ. As we target the enemy in warfare prayer, it is as if we are a sculptor, surveying a lump of rock. The sculptor can envisage in his mind's eye the beautiful sculpture that will emerge, and begins to chip off the rock all that is unwanted, which prevents the sculpture from being seen in all its glory. The attention of the artist is not upon the pieces of rock he chips off, but upon the emerging shape of the sculpture. This is the focus that the Christian needs to maintain, as he or she weighs into the spiritual battle: not the demons that need to be dealt with, so much as the emerging shape of the beautiful sculpture that is currently obscured by the demonic. Is this not what intercession – standing in the gap – is all about? Seeing the situation as it now is, the situation as God wants it to be and closing the gap between the two through prayer.

Now there is a great danger in being ill-informed about the nature of the demonic – Acts 19:13–16 is a good example of operating outside of one's level of expertise and standing in Christ. Just as the sculptor needs to understand the nature of the rock he is using – where its fault lines lie, how best to strike it and so on – we need to inform ourselves regarding the nature of the demonic, about low-level spirits and how they are controlled by 'strongmen', about territorial spirits, and about which spirits seem to group together, such as the spirits of Jezebel (control) and witchcraft, with their lower-level companions, fear and despondency. However, the sculptor is not judged on his knowledge of rock, but on the sculpture he produces, and in spiritual terms, our effectiveness in Spiritual Warfare is not judged on our expert knowledge of the demonic, but on the growth of a Christ-like nature within us. This is not merely playing with words – it is the difference between presenting the returning Christ with an encyclopaedia of useful information on rocks, and presenting Him with a beautiful, blemish-free sculpture. He knows all about rocks – it's the sculpture He's interested in!

Keep a right balance

We are very cautious at Kingfisher of anyone who claims to have a 'deliverance ministry'. Not that we don't believe in the validity of the need to bring deliverance to those who are oppressed by unclean spirits, but because it tends to suggest an unbalanced understanding of the kind of ministry people need. Whilst it is undoubtedly true that many people are oppressed by these unclean spirits, it is equally true that many, many more need healing from past hurts and traumas. To speak too glibly about praying for deliverance can be unhelpful and damaging. In our experience, it is always best to start from the position of not assuming that someone is demonised – indeed that is often the last option that we go for. However, a repeated pattern of sinful behaviour can and often does lead to voluntary or involuntary oppression by a demonic spirit. The difference between these two types of oppression is important.

Involuntary oppression

Often, when someone has experienced sexual abuse as a child, there are implications that surface later in life, which seem to be unrelated to the original violation. We have come across those with eating disorders, those who have become consumed with sexual immorality, those who now struggle with their sexuality. Often what has occurred is that, at the time of the sexual abuse, an unclean spirit has entered into that person, the effect of which is to bring about the above-mentioned problems in later life. This is termed an involuntary oppression, for obvious reasons – the person was the victim of abuse, which led, beyond their control to allowing an unclean spirit to enter. Do they need ministry? Certainly, but not just to have the 'demon of lust', or the 'spirit of bulimia' cast out. They need healing from the trauma and violation of the abuse they suffered, and also to have the unclean spirit lifted from their spirit. They also need to release forgiveness to those who have caused these subsequent problems. This requires teaching on what forgiveness actually means – not 'letting someone off the hook', saying it doesn't matter any more, or saying it doesn't hurt any more. Rather forgiveness is about a decision – a decision to no longer be linked to the other person in bitterness and hurt. Forgiveness is about making the decision to give to God the responsibility of sorting the other person out. It is a matter of being honest with God about the hurt, but deciding to no longer carry the cancer of unforgiveness, but rather to entrust the situation to God, for him to bring justice. Forgiveness is about a decision to walk free, which, in turn, unlocks other areas of hurt and pain in the person's life.

Voluntary oppression

There are many things we choose to do – like, for instance, 'dabbling' with Tarot cards, or ouija boards – of our own free will, which have unforeseen, frightening consequences. These are voluntary acts that lead to oppression, and they need to be renounced and repented of. Renunciation is about the intent not to walk in those ways in the future, whilst repentance is about bringing the past to God for him to deal with. Only after both renunciation and repentance does the unclean spirit lose its legal right to inhabit the person, and can then be told to leave.

It is so important in the area of Spiritual Warfare to exercise discernment. You cannot heal a demon or cast out a past hurt! Neither can sin be rehabilitated as demonic oppression – sin is still sin, even in the trendy nineties! It is important, therefore to teach new Christians at an early stage to keep a right and healthy balance in Spiritual Warfare – to not try to cast out everything that isn't nailed down, but to be aware that, where there is emotional, spiritual, moral or physical weakness, there is likely to be the demonic lurking. If you leave your car door unlocked overnight with the keys in the ignition, the chances of the vehicle being stolen are greatly increased. It may not be, the first night, but the longer it is left in that condition, the greater the likelihood that, sooner or later, it will disappear. Likewise in the spiritual realm. The greatest defence against Satan is to take the keys out of the car and lock the door – in other words, pursue Christlikeness: submit to God. Draw close to him and he will draw close to you. Resist Satan and he will flee from you!

Keep practising

The results of Spiritual Warfare are often unseen, which can lead to discouragement and disbelief. For instance, when Kingfisher moved to its current premises in the middle of an estate with a lot of social problems, we prayed a great deal over the area. We prayed that the forces of darkness – the fear, the violence and the lawlessness – would be bound in the name of Jesus, and the Spirit of God would begin to permeate the streets and the houses on the estate. How can you measure the effectiveness of that kind of prayer? It didn't seem to result in people coming to us and begging to be told what they must do to inherit eternal life, so maybe it was all just hot air!

It was not until three years later, when a policeman started attending the church and became a Christian, that we began to perceive the effects of that warfare. 'Coinciding' with our arrival on that estate, there was a large-scale police operation that resulted in the arrest and conviction of all the main drug barons and thugs. The realisation of this challenged us, not only to keep praying, but to believe more in the reality of the unseen battle that is being waged in the heavenly realms, and its outworking here in the real world. Keep persevering in warfare prayer – it really works!

Keep teaching

I am sometimes alarmed at the rather extreme positions that new Christians take on the subject of Spiritual Warfare. It can seem that having a 'bad hair' day can be ascribed to Satan 'having a go', and as for a married couple having a row – well, that's **definitely** the devil having a field day! Faced with these often wild interpretations of what is happening in life, the temptation for many a minister is to discourage any development in the area of Spiritual Warfare, and to put it down to the pursuit of the lunatic fringe. However, as has been mentioned earlier, the correction for abuse is not disuse, but correct use. Consequently, at Kingfisher we have developed a series of seminars, carefully researched and well balanced, that take people through all aspects of Spiritual Warfare, Setting the Captives Free, Healing through Deliverance, healing from Rejection, and so on. We encourage all members of the church to attend these seminars, partly so that everyone can receive ministry if they need it, but also so that the 'Chinese Whispers' syndrome is firmly knocked on the head. Everyone is taught on these key subjects by people we have trained and that we trust. Everyone hears the same teaching. Everyone is equipped to begin to discern what is going on, not only in their own lives, but in the lives of those around them. Spiritual Warfare is not a specialist subject to be practised only by the few – it is intended that **all** members of the body pursue Christlikeness ... that everyone has the extraneous bits of rock chipped off, and that we are all presented spotless and clean before the returning Bridegroom.

Evaluation points

- What have been your experiences, both positive and negative, in the area of Spiritual Warfare?
- What would you say was the primary focus in your church? Is it to become like Christ, or are other things more important?
- In what ways could Spiritual Warfare be introduced to your church, so that it would become a normal part of church life? Do you agree that this is an essential part of church life? If not, why not?

Chapter 9

The God Who Keeps His Word

The phone rang at one of those inconvenient times. It was Jan's turn to answer it, and I have to admit, I hoped it was for her. After a few moments, she came to find me and handed me the phone with a rather surprised look on her face. 'It's for you – it's Willow Creek Community Church!' Well, we have various practical jokers in our church, and I was pretty sure I knew which one it was, so I took the phone and let this person know what I thought about practical jokers who rang their Pastor up just when he'd got to the end of a long and hard day! There was a pause at the other end of the line, followed by the voice of a rather surprised American, who introduced himself as Jim Schiltz, a volunteer in the International Ministries department of Willow Creek Community Church. My immediate prayer, 'Lord, if you're going to come back again, now might be a good time!' seemed to go unanswered, so I attempted to repair some of the damage and start again. Willow Creek were looking to send a team of people to the UK for some oversees experience, and they had heard of Kingfisher, so would we like a team of ten people! I had to restrain myself from asking him to post them down the telephone line there and then

– of course we would like a team from Willow Creek! Jim suggested I might like to pray about it with the eldership and I said 'Of course, that goes without saying!' The eldership and the church were as enthusiastic as I was, and several months later, we were at the airport to greet a wonderful group of Americans. What followed was an incredible week of God restoring, healing, opening doors and bringing about things He had long since promised. The week culminated with a major one-day conference, with church leaders from all over the UK attending. As I stood at the back of the auditorium at the start of the conference and watched hundreds of people worshipping God, led by Kingfisher's superb worship group, I felt overcome with emotion. Just a few years ago, fired by a conference run by Willow Creek, a dozen ordinary people had committed themselves to building a church that would reach lost people and be a place where people could experience transformation. We didn't have any money, or any credibility, or any backing. We did, however, have a calling from a great God – a God who promised to lead us, to guide us and to build His Church. As I stood at the back of that conference, I realised that God's promises are not just hot air – they are true. If God has promised something, He will deliver, far more abundantly than we can ask or even imagine. I never imagined, in 1992, as I left that Willow Creek Conference in Birmingham fired with a passion to do something similar in the UK, that the Lord would engineer events such that, four years later, that very church would come and visit us! What an incredibly extravagant God we have, using one of America's largest churches to encourage an ordinary, fairly small church in England.

We realise that God has barely begun with us at Kingfisher – we have only just crossed the starting line.

But in the few, short years we have been in existence, we have been reminded, time and time again, that Jesus Christ, through the local church, is the one, true hope for humanity. Hopeless existences have been transformed from a Christless eternity, into hope-filled, empowered, joyful lives. God has poured His extravagant love on us time and time again, achieving things that we dared not even ask. For example, the management team of Kingfisher Ministries met three nights ago to discuss the future. One of the projects on the table for discussion was the next music album to be produced. The desire was to produce this album on CD to a professional standard. As we reviewed the costs involved, we realised that it was currently beyond our reach, and so we agreed to put the project on the back burner and do it as-and-when the finances became available. The meeting ended at 11pm, and Judith, one of directors of Kingfisher Ministries arrived home shortly after that. As she went through her front door, the phone was ringing. A Recording Engineer had been out walking that evening, and had been stopped by God, who convicted him that he had to ring Judith (whose husband, Mike, he had met once), and offer his recording studio (one of the best in the land) and his time for free. It transpired that God was talking to him about this at the very time that we were discussing the project in the meeting! Truly, He is able to do immeasurably more than we ask or imagine! Now is the time we are called to dream great dreams and have visions that seem to exceed our wildest expectations. This is a time of immense and sustained outpouring of the Holy Spirit. Is it all to be hoarded by the already-convinced, or is God raising up those with the passion of John Knox, who said, 'Give me Scotland, or I die!', or the zeal of Hudson Taylor, who desired nothing more than 'to spend and be spent for Him who died for me. I feel as if for this I could give up everything, every idol, however dear'[1]

There is nothing this world needs more than the saving work of Jesus Christ, and there is no more compelling testimony to that work of Christ than a biblically functioning local community of Christians, who have vision, who care enough about that vision to be strategic about its fulfilment, and who are committed to seeing lives transformed. This world needs the local church! If the local church is not fishing for the King, then what is it about?

Has God lit your blue touch paper with a vision for what Church could be like? He is a God who keeps His word. The smallness of your congregation is not a barrier. The smallness of your church budget is not going to frustrate God's plans. Your lack of stature in the local community cannot limit God. If He has lit your blue touch paper with a vision that will bring glory to His name, extend His Kingdom and reach the spiritually lost with the life-transforming message of the Gospel, then no force, on earth or in the spiritual realms is going to stop it.

The crucial issue is this: Are we willing to pay the price? Are our lives laid down for the cause of Christ? Are we willing to do what it takes to be used mightily by God. How will we answer the question that has come down the ages, and is still as urgent today as it was nearly three thousand years ago:

'Whom shall I send? And who will go for us?'

(Isaiah 6:8)

Endnotes

Chapter 1

1. Marshall Broomhall, *The Man Who Believed God ... The Story of Hudson Taylor*, China Inland Mission, 1959, p. 6
2. Quoted in *The Daily Telegraph*, July 12th, 1988
3. Quoted in his speach at the Labour Party Conference, Chesterfield, June 11th, 1988

Chapter 2

1. Chris Bonnington, *The Quest for Adventure*, Book Club Associates, 1982, p. 56

Chapter 5

1. Juan Carlos Ortiz, quoted in *Discipleship*, David Watson, Hodder and Stoughton, 1981, p. 68
2. David Watson, *Discipleship* Hodder and Stoughton, 1981, p. 16
3. David Watson, *op cit*, p. 18

Chapter 6

1. Carl F. George, *How to Break Growth Barriers*, Baker Book House, 1993, p. 19
2. Lee Strobel, *What Jesus Would Say*, Zondervan, 1994, p. 92
3. D. Johnson and J. VanVonderen, *The Subtle Power of Spiritual Abuse*, Bethany House Publishers, 1991
4. Based upon a talk given by Clive Corfield, Ellel Ministries, 1996

Chapter 7

1. Carl F. George, *op cit*, p. 186

Chapter 9

1. Marshall Broomhall, *op cit*, p. 34